BEYOND THE BROKEN GLASS SLIPPER

Queen Esther

QUEEN ESTHER

Beyond the Broken Glass Slipper

First published by Queen Scripts LLC
https://queenscripts.wixsite.com/my-site
queenscripts@gmail.com 2022

First edition

ISBN: 9798218021467

Editing by Shelley Mascia
Advisor: Inspiring Honey Publishing LLC
Typesetting by Inspiring Honey Publishing LLC
Cover art by Be Celebrated Printing

This book was professionally typeset on Reedsy.
Find out more at reedsy.com

To all the women of God who have endured a crushing of a hope, a shattering of a dream, a breaking of a vision– In seemingly broken times, these devotions are for you.

Queen Esther

Contents

Foreword

Years ago, I told a friend that I felt like God was calling me to write a book. I didn't know where to start. She suggested the title "Beyond the Broken Glass." Something in my spirit stirred, though, to name this book "Beyond the Broken Glass Slipper." My original plan was that each chapter would be inspired by a fairy tale. Because of this decision (and my unwillingness to sacrifice and seek direction), I was blocked for the longest time. So, the draft lay dormant. I have since seen the error of my ways. My inspiration is not to be from fairy tales, but every chapter is inspired by the Word of God. Some chapters may allude to fairy tales as parables that help get the point across. The point of this book is for women to know that there is more to this life than what is in front of us. What God has in store for you is more than you have envisioned as the perfect life in your mind. Your own creative fairy tale for yourself is not what God wants you to seek Him for. Yes, we are allowed to dream. But we must first yield to God and His will for our lives. His purpose is what should drive the next path we take. Don't lay dormant like this book did. Study and meditate on the Word of God to make moves toward your destiny-the way I am doing right now. In the final draft of this book, I am torn and tattered in my spirit, not understanding why some things are not going the way I thought they would. This morning, it just came to me that my current glass slipper must be shattered, broken—for me to pour out what God is speaking to us. In the middle of my fragmented glass pieces that I know I have no power to piece together, I pray for you, my sisters, and for myself. God will help all of us move past these fractured seasons in life and give us vision to see that there is something more. He has something more, something past this, something on the other side of this, something beyond this broken glass slipper. My prayer is that through our tears in the broken places, we see in the supernatural what is beyond, and don't stop until we reach it.

-Queen Esther

I

INTRODUCTION

DEVOTION 1:A CHILD IS BORN

Jeremiah 1: 4-5 Now the word of the Lord came to me saying, "Before I formed you in the womb I knew you, and before you were born I consecrated you; I have appointed you a prophet to the nations." (New American Standard Bible)

In the movie "The Never Ending Story," a young boy, Bastian, read a book with the same title about a land called Fantasia. He is so engrossed with the characters that he is pulled into the plot. In the story, there is a void of darkness called "The Nothing" that is eating away the land of Fantasia. The Childlike Empress, the ruler of Fantasia, is dying in the Ivory Tower due to The Nothing. A young warrior boy, Atreyu, has been called upon to seek out a discovery that will end The Nothing. After traveling through many perils, Atreyu arrives at the Ivory Tower disappointed to tell the Empress that he failed at his mission.

However, the Empress informs him that he has succeeded in his mission. He has brought the human child reading the book along with him through the story. The human child reading the book, Bastian, is then revealed as the "Golden Child" to save Fantasia. If he calls a new name for the Princess before The Nothing consumes the Ivory Tower, Fantasia is saved. He names her Moonchild. With Bastian's imagination, Fantasia is restored.

Isn't it something that a kingdom could be saved from such an ordinary boy? This boy has no special powers, but as fate would have it, he runs into this particular bookstore and retrieves this specific book, leading to fulfilling his destiny. Saving a kingdom—what a destiny!

The life we live is not a fairy tale. You must understand this reality—**there is something greater than fate at work in your life.** It is God's perfect plan for His Kingdom! Do you know that you were divinely created to fulfill a specific mission on Earth? Do you know that He had something great in mind just for you before you were born? God put you on Earth for a mission that no one can complete but you.

Psalm 139:14 reads, " I will praise thee; for I am fearfully and wonderfully made: marvelous are thy works; and that my soul knoweth right well."

Before I was formed in my mother's womb, He called me. There are several facets to the call in my life. But as I am writing this book, I am stepping out blindly, not knowing the entire purpose of my writing it, where it will go, who it will reach, or who it will touch. I am answering a call that I know "this child" was born to fulfill. Someone reading this book is much like me, feeling too mediocre to answer the call of destiny on your life. I encourage you to BELIEVE!

Despite your complexion-clear or bumpy, light or dark; despite your hair texture-coarse or fine, thick or thin, short or long. Despite your body build-pear shaped, straight up and down, little on the bottom and big on top with little legs. Do you not know that you are remarkable??

Nothing, and I mean, NOTHING that He made was not good. Come to the realization that the child born within you has a great destiny that you may not realize or seems unfathomable. BUT it's there. That child has been in the womb long enough. It's time to deliver! There is an old Dr. Watts song from the traditional black church that says,

A charge to keep I have
A God to glorify A never-dying soul to save And fit it for the sky
To serve this present age
My calling to fulfill O, may it all my power engage
To do my Master's will!

What is the will of your Master? Do you think He took time to pair 23 sets of chromosomes together, choose which genes would be dominant and which ones would be recessive, and allow you to experience all that you have until this very moment just for you not to act on what He created you for in His purpose?? Don't dare take this precious gift of life that He gave you any longer without fulfilling what you were born to do!! Allow the gift inside of you to be born!!

Let's Pray...

Father God, I come to you right now, giving you praise and glory for being God! We acknowledge you as the Sovereign God! The Master

Creator! God, we thank you for taking the time to think about us when you had Creation on your mind! Thank you, God, for considering us! Thank you, God, for orchestrating our lives for your purpose! Help us never forget how special we are to you. Help us never forget that you would not have taken the time to create us if we did not hold a special place in you. We cast out any spirits of depression, low self-esteem, insecurity, suicide, and any other mental illness, for we know that any thoughts that have us thinking of ourselves as 'less than' are ill and do not mix with your Word. As we attempt to move closer to you, Lord, reveal to us, your children, the purpose for which we were born. Show us glimpses along the way, Lord. Help us to take in more of you. We are careful to give you all praise, glory, and honor, Lord! In the name of Jesus Christ, we pray. Amen

II

PROCESS

DEVOTION 2: ARE YOU AT LEAST SEEKING?

Matthew 2:1-2 Now when Jesus was born in Bethlehem of Judaea in the days of Herod the king, behold, there came wise men from the east to Jerusalem, Saying, "Where is he that is born King of the Jews? For we have seen his star in the east, and are come to worship him."
(King James Version)

In "The Wizard of Oz", Dorothy from Kansas and her little dog, Toto, are caught up in a cyclone and find themselves in the Land of Oz. Oz is not where Dorothy wants to be. Dorothy wants to find her way back home. The Munchkins tell her there is one who can help her, the Great Wizard of Oz. He can be found if she follows the yellow brick road to the Emerald City. And so, Dorothy sets out on the yellow brick road.

Dorothy could have chosen to stay with the Munchkins and pine away. They, perhaps, could have helped keep her safe from the Wicked Witch of the West. However, the Land of Oz is not where she is supposed to be. So, she gathers the courage to journey into the unknown, seeking the answer to what is in her heart.

I am reminded of the Wise Men from the East who came to Jerusalem seeking Jesus. They saw an extraordinary star. The presence of this star stirred them to pack bags, load up camels, prepare for desert and various terrains, and move them to set out on a long journey to another country for the opportunity to worship the Child King of the Jews. They weren't even Jews themselves, and yet the star symbolizing this child's birth sparked within them to set out on a search for the Christ Child. They had no idea what the forecast was going to be nor what dangers they might face on the way. All they knew was that a Savior was being born, and they had to bring offerings, pay respect and tribute, and worship.

What about us?

Are we at least trying to seek our Savior? Are we at least trying to seek God's destiny for us in this season? Is there anything within us that we see or feel, a star the Holy Spirit has revealed worth our effort to seek?

Do not live your life never seeking God and His desire for you. He fearfully and wondrously made us, and we have a charge to keep. We know that we are to witness Christ to mankind. But what is your specific role in the kingdom?

Jeremiah 29:11 states, "For I know the plans I have for you," declares the LORD, "plans to prosper you and not to harm you, plans to give you hope and a future." (New International Version)

It is God who knows the plans, God that can see to you prospering, God that can reveal it to you. Are you on the yellow brick road at least *trying* to find Him? I wasted so many years not taking the effort to try to seek Him like I should have!

What does it cost us? An extra 15-30 minutes of sleep in the morning instead of hitting the snooze button, having devotion with him? We can record The Haves and the Have Nots and Housewives of Whoever to make sure we don't miss an episode, but how many of us record at least one show a week on TBN or The WORD Network not to miss out on this week's Rhema word from God for us?

Sitting up under my pastor on Sunday and Wednesday nights is the first word I hear, for I know he has my spiritual diet. But I know I must also target what else I allow to filter my system during the week. Before church apps and so many Social Media live options, I started a practice a few years ago where I would record Bishop G.E. Patterson, Bishop T.D. Jakes, then Bishop Noel Jones on Sundays.

That was enough recordings to take me Monday through Wednesday with the extra Word. Bishop Jakes was also on Monday-Friday. No matter what other shows I recorded that I wanted to watch after getting off work, I would turn on one of these recordings in my room as I fell asleep. Honestly, I'm not 100% true to this practice, but I do credit this as one of the things that has been the fuel to help me start on this journey-seeking more of His word.

I don't know about you, but Satan constantly tries to infiltrate my mind. Because of this, I feel it necessary to try to pour The Word into my last thoughts before going to sleep. I must admit I was becoming so engaged with others' sermons, I was replacing that with my daily study in the Word, which was not good. I had to go back and spend time in devotion and reading the Word for my personal relationship with God. You must make the effort to do WHATEVER is necessary to keep your mind set on seeking God and His will for your life.

The Wise Men had no idea the impact they would have on God's kingdom. Centuries later, they appear on Christmas cards and Nativity scenes. Songs, dramas, and sermons galore have been written about them. And all because they stepped out and moved on what was stirring within them.

Have you thought about the fact that they have been famous for centuries, and yet, the Biblical Scripture doesn't mention their names? It's not their names that are important, but the part they play in the kingdom. So don't live your life for the purpose of getting your name out there. Make sure what you do is for the purpose of edifying Him and not you, and you will succeed.

Still don't know what to do? Try this.

Start seeking!

Let's Pray…

Lord, I come to you right now asking for divine guidance for my sisters and me. We do not know which way to go. We could make many steps, but our desire is for our actions to be in line with your will. We seek your help, Lord. Show us the way. You said in Jeremiah 33 that if we called upon you, you would answer us. You said you would show us great and mighty things that we do not know. Speak to our hearts and allow your Word to be a lamp unto our feet and a light unto our path. Like the Wise Men, we don't know what lies ahead, but help us to trust in you to route us the way we need to go. We are weaklings without you, but warriors with you! Meet us where we are on this journey right now and lead us like the Shepherd we know you are. We take no pride in any steps we make, for as always, all honor and glory belong to you, Lord. We pray in the name of Jesus. Amen.

DEVOTION 3:STOP WORRYING ABOUT YOUR OUTSIDE PACKAGE

Micah 5:2 But you, O Bethlehem Ephrathah, who are too little to be among the clans of Judah, from you shall come forth for me one who is to be ruler in Israel, whose coming forth is from of old, from ancient days.
(English Standard Version)

One of the silliest fairy tales I remember is that of The Princess and the Pea. A prince traveled near and far to find a princess. He comes across many of them, but something is always wrong with them. They appear to not be real princesses.

One stormy night, a young lady claiming to be a princess knocks on the palace gate seeking shelter. She says she's a princess, but the wind and rain have done her in! Hair tattered, clothes drenched, water seeping out of her shoes, she looks a hot mess! Her appearance seems so awful that the queen makes a move to test if she is really a princess or not. Legend had it that a real princess has skin so delicate that she could not sleep on a pea, so the queen lays a pea under 20 mattresses for the princess to lay on. When morning comes, the princess is questioned how she slept. She states she barely slept and tossed and turned all night until she was black and blue. This revealed that she was an actual princess. So, the prince married her, and they lived happily ever after.

In the Bible, Micah makes mention of the city of Bethlehem being overlooked because of her small size but prophesies greatness. Calamity was headed for the nation of Israel. Still, Micah gave Israel hope in the coming of the Messiah from this city.

He speaks to Bethlehem in the 2nd verse of Micah's 5th chapter saying, "Hey, Bethlehem! I know I've sounded for all the troops to gather from all the clans of Judah, and as a city, you are so little, you aren't even numbered among the clans of Judah. However, you won't be noted as insignificant for long. Out of you, little old Bethlehem, a ruler shall come forth, The Ancient of Days, from everlasting to everlasting. All Israel will be blessed because of you."

Could such greatness really come from a place as small as Bethlehem? Bethlehem was so tiny that in the book of Nehemiah, it isn't even listed as a city of Judah. But what looked insignificant from the outside held eternal purpose.

What makes you feel minor or insignificant? Is it your family history? Is it your educational status or job title? Is it your look-too light or dark, too skinny or fat, wrong shape, or hair? Is it that in whatever your gift is-writing, singing, dancing, real estate, design-you're not looked upon as having achieved as high a level as you feel others have?

I can write about this because, as a woman, I have thought these things about myself. I have constantly made statements:

- *"I know I can't sing like so-and-so..."*
- *"I know I can't dance like so-and-so..."*
- *"God didn't bless me with a shape that Social Media and entertainment applauds..."*
- *"I'm not light-skinned like my sisters and the rest of my family...*
"

BUT GOD...He so fearfully and marvelously made me that I had to quit looking at what I thought was lacking and made me feel insignificant. There was something on the inside working in superior to my outside-Hallelujah!-that held eternal purpose and made me significant in the Kingdom.

Your credit may be messed up now, your job not the best, your family situation tore up from the floor up...BUT if you know **who** you are, when you are put to the test (like the Princess), **who you are in eternity** will be revealed. Our God is so amazing that not one thing He put together is insignificant in His plan. This includes you and me!

Remember the work of the chromosome pairing? Why are there some genes He let be dominant while others lie recessive? Why let your childhood and adult life twist on a path to bring you to this point at this specific time in your life? Trust me, He had a reason, and it is **significant!**

You are *significant!*

The more you continue to seek Him, the more what He put on your inside will shine through to your outside. Note that the Princess didn't have to put herself out there on the line with a big sign saying, "Hey, I'm a Princess!" But, in due time, it was shown. And she wasn't even at her best in all her purposed glory when it happened either.

Whether at church, on your job, or in relationships, stop worrying about your outside package not being enough. If you consistently put yourself out there on Social Media to show how pretty or sexy you are, you frequently make statements about who is jealous of you, or you have to let people know when you buy this and that. **NEWSFLASH:** Your inside must not be about nothing!

It must take the outer, material things and responses from man to make you feel as if you are of some substance. Because if your inside was all that, you wouldn't have to advertise to people all these things about you or seek confirmation that you are who you are portraying to be. They'd already know your worth!

You may not be where you want to be, but the important thing is being where He wants you to be. You don't have to jump through hoops to get where He wants you to be. He doesn't need your help, either. He'll do it in His timing. You've got to trust that.

It was 700 years after Micah's prophecy before Christ was born in Bethlehem. And thousands of years later, we're still singing

"O Little Town of Bethlehem." The eternal significance of her place in the Kingdom still reigns. I'm not saying to leave your outside undone, but make sure your inside overshadows your outside. His eternal destiny takes care of the rest.

Let's Pray...

Father God, I come pleading for my sisters. As women, we can get so caught up in physical and external attributes that it can make us insecure and even jealous. Sometimes it may not be physical attributes but where our status is or what we do not have that make us feel this way. Lord, we know you are the God who uses foolish things to confound the wise. Whatever we may deem as insignificant on the outside is just enough because of what you have placed inside us. Each of us, as believers, have your Holy Spirit and can access power from on high. Help us to see ourselves the way you see us. Help us to see the beauty of how we are made in your image. Help us to recognize the princess on the inside of each of us, for you, our Father, are the King of Kings. Send any insecurity, depression, or thoughts of insignificance back to Hell from whence they came. Let royal spirits arise in my sisters so that they may walk in your eternal divine purpose. In Jesus' name, we ask these things. Amen.

DEVOTION 4:PUZZLE PIECES

Acts 9:10-16 In Damascus there was a disciple named Ananias. The Lord called to him in a vision, "Ananias!" "Yes, Lord," he answered. The Lord told him, "Go to the house of Judas on Straight Street and ask for a man from Tarsus named Saul, for he is praying. In a vision he has seen a man named Ananias come and place his hands on him to restore his sight." "Lord," Ananias answered, "I have heard many reports about this man and all the harm he has done to your holy people in Jerusalem. And he has come here with authority from the chief priests to arrest all who call on your name." But the Lord said to Ananias, "Go! This man is my chosen instrument to proclaim my name to the Gentiles and their kings and to the people of Israel. I will show him how much he must suffer for my name." (New International Version)

As I was going to work, I was meditating on my family members. On both sides of my family, the previous generation is shaped by various experiences: not being raised by biological parents, but by extended family – loved, yet there was a void; the 'outside' child in the family; family secrets of childhood abuse, and so on.

When I think of these individuals, the pieces of each one's puzzle are different. Universally, the sharp curves and straight lines are in different places for everyone. In other words, life's cuts and angles shape who we are. That shape may cause one to respond with certain behaviors others deem unfeasible. So before unfairly getting upset with our parents, spouses, friends, etc. over their actions, consider the shape of who they are.

Each person's puzzle makeup is so complex that sometimes we expect too much of people by not realizing WHO they are-how all the ingredients of their past, experiences, and genetics combine. Each combination yields different levels, depths of strength, love, and support they can give depending on what is going on in their lives. We may be expecting a certain depth of support from one, and we don't know internally what they are dealing with and their ability to support us when they are struggling.

When that person-mother, father, sister, brother, friend-isn't the rock we need, we often become bitter and angry with them, and it causes separation in relationships. We are all flawed in some way or another. Broken. Lost. Jaded. But we cannot operate alone. We are just like puzzle pieces.

Have you ever seen a puzzle piece in the shape of a complete circle that contains the whole picture within itself? No! It takes all the pieces coming together before the image can be seen with all its beauty. And even though it may exist, I have never come across a puzzle with one piece to it. Each piece is unique, and only one piece can fit in any perspective space. No matter how much you try to force a piece in a spot that looks like it should fit, it will not work.

Often, we try to fit people in spots where we want them, but it does not work because God has not shaped that person to be in that spot in your life. Unfortunately, I have made that mistake many a time! So, I had to learn to leave some spaces void until God put the puzzle piece where He wanted it to be.

In **Acts**, we study Ananias, a believer of Jesus Christ. God speaks to him and tells him to go to Strait Street and find Saul of Tarsus. God wants Ananias to pray for him and lay hands on him so that he might receive his sight. Ananias is appalled by what God is asking him. Saul of Tarsus? Really, God? You must've not heard about him. Let me inform you of who this man is (as if God doesn't know). He says, God, this man has letters of authority to kill the believers! It's probably good he's blind. Let him stay blind! I know you don't want me to go lay hands on him! But God gives Ananias an emphatic, Go! Do as I told you. He is MY instrument. I chose him, and he will proclaim my name to Gentiles, Kings, and all of Israel.

So Ananias moved and did as God said. Who would've thought that Saul, the killer of those who called on the name of Jesus, would end up being the most prolific preacher of all times? Who knew that there was a Paul inside of a Saul? Only God knew. And God knew it would take someone with complex, jagged edges to fulfill the task He had set.

Sitting under Rabbi Gamaliel, having astute knowledge of the scriptures, being a Roman citizen, and all the experiences that made Paul were needed on his journey. In his first letter to

Timothy, Paul explains the grace of Christ by saying that he was the chief of sinners. If God could save him, anyone who truly believed in Jesus' name could receive the same grace and eternal life.

There are two things I want you to get out of this devotion. One is that no one is greater than any other. When dealing with relationships, recognize their sharp and rounded edges for what they are, and love them. You do not have any power to shape anyone into being firm where you want, soft where you want, or leaning the way you want them to. Only God can do that. Love them in the shape they are now and do not try to push them where they do not fit. If there is a void, let God fill that space and let Him place who He knows will perfectly fit your empty spaces. Yes, He knows better than you who will fit that space, for He is the one who is the artist in the first place. He has knowledge that you don't have. Trust Him to fill your empty space with the right person at the right time.

The second thing is to forgive those who haven't fit where you wanted them to. I know people who have held bitterness inside their hearts for friends and family, even parents, because they weren't a specified piece of the puzzle. Sometimes God removes the people because their season is over. They may have been an anchor piece in the past but are not beneficial to you now.

Sometimes God has ordained someone else to be an anchor piece during this current season, or perhaps, God wants to be the anchor piece! Instead of having this person to vent to and lean on, God wants you to vent to Him and lean on Him. He may be leaving a space void so that He can fill your life before

He attaches the piece to you. Maybe it's you who needs your edges molded before He allows you to mess up who He will connect to you.

You may be the one with the jagged edges that need rounding! You have been sharp and caused hurt in someone else's life at some point in your life, so don't play the victim. Most importantly, don't let Satan use your broken places to make you feel like an inconsiderable piece of the puzzle. Just as God used Paul, He can and will use you. Every hurt, hard, broken, soft edge or curve of you-give it to the Master and let Him mold you. It is all a necessary part of the process. Pray right now.

Let's Pray…

Lord, I am a mess. I am broken. I am lost. I am hard. I am hurt. I am weak. Please put me on your potter's wheel. You are the potter. I am the clay. Make me over again. Lay your hands on me, Jesus! I don't mind! I don't mind because I know that You are the author and finisher of my faith. You know the end from the beginning. It is You who will perfect those things concerning me and You who has plans to prosper me, giving me a future and a hope. Help me recognize the spot where you have placed others in my life and help me be the best puzzle piece you have me to be where you placed me. In the name of Jesus, I submit my clay to You. Amen.

DEVOTION 5: LADY IN WAITING–PART I

Esther 2: 8-9, 12-18 When the king's order and edict had been proclaimed, many young women were brought to the citadel of Susa and put under the care of Hegai. Esther also was taken to the king's palace and entrusted to Hegai, who had charge of the harem. She pleased him and won his favor. Immediately he provided her with her beauty treatments and special food. He assigned to her seven female attendants selected from the king's palace and moved her and her attendants into the best place in the harem… Before a young woman's turn came to go in to King Xerxes, she had to complete twelve months of beauty treatments prescribed for the women, six months with oil of myrrh and six with perfumes and cosmetics. And this is how she would go to the king: Anything she wanted was given her to take with her from the harem to the king's palace. In the evening she would go there and in the morning return to another part of the harem to the care of Shaashgaz, the king's eunuch who was in charge of the concubines. She would not return to the king unless he was pleased with her and summoned her by name. When the turn came for Esther (the young woman Mordecai had adopted, the daughter of his uncle Abihail) to go to the king, she asked for nothing other than

what Hegai, the king's eunuch who was in charge of the harem, suggested. And Esther won the favor of everyone who saw her. She was taken to King Xerxes in the royal residence in the tenth month, the month of Tebeth, in the seventh year of his reign. Now the king was attracted to Esther more than to any of the other women, and she won his favor and approval more than any of the other virgins. So he set a royal crown on her head and made her queen instead of Vashti. And the king gave a great banquet, Esther's banquet, for all his nobles and officials. He proclaimed a holiday throughout the provinces and distributed gifts with royal liberality.
(New International Version)

I love to watch movies set in medieval times. There is something about royal women that intrigue me. I have heard the term "ladies-in-waiting" and knew somewhat about what they were, but before writing this devotion, I decided to do some research.

There are variations for this role from country to country, yet this one thing can be stated. Historically, ladies-in-waiting were women of nobility who held a position in court where they 'waited' on and served a higher-ranking noblewoman, such as a queen. They made the bathwater, gave massages with fragrances and oils, dressed, brushed hair, and did the bidding for their mistress. A lady-in-waiting had to be educated, schooled in the ways of court life, etiquette, and how to present with a manner of grace and culture above those of ordinary women in the kingdom.

However, I do not intend for you to consider yourself above some, yet below, any other woman in rank. On the contrary,

I intend for you to consider yourself of nobility, no doubt, for we are a royal priesthood. Your father is the King of Kings. You are, though, considered a servant to only one, and that one is Jesus Christ.

Have you ever felt like you are a lady in waiting? I have! I have felt like a lady waiting on time to bring about a change and waiting on others (serving) but never getting served in return. What have you felt like you were waiting on? A job opportunity? A ministry move? A husband? A child? Waiting on something that you have no control over…it all depends on whether favor falls your way or not.

When it comes to favor, you have no control over when or if favor will fall the way you want it to, but one thing you need to do is be prepared for it to fall. So often we sit in a cloud of depression, wondering if, or when, the bloom will ever manifest in our lives. It certainly doesn't help when we see others reap the manifestation of the same thing we are waiting for. Sometimes, we don't feel like they have gone through half of what we went through in prayer and preparation for it.

A lady in waiting must realize that we all have our own yellow brick roads to travel before we reach our Emerald City as a woman of God. Our God, who is Omniscient, has His reason for our route to be what it is for His purpose. Your waiting involves serving until the proper time for your elevation. You are a servant to Christ, and whatever it is that is your desire - it must fit not just your desire for your life, but it must fit His will and purpose for His kingdom.

I urge you to consider other women of God. Rachel was loved more than Leah, as Hannah was loved more than Peninnah. Both Rachel and Hannah felt a void for a child, and their yellow brick roads were paths laid for thousands, possibly millions, of women to grab as a resource of how to hold on in their wait. Ruth and Rahab had a yearning to be connected to the God of Israel they had come to know. They were willing to forsake their home, nationality, and religion to go on an adventure with Yahweh to see where their path would lead.

The moves they made took them on unknown journeys. They waited to see what life would be like and how it would prosper them to adjoin themselves to the One True God. Ruth just desired to be with Naomi, and Rahab just desired to save her family. Both felt an urge in their spiritual womb to step out on faith and see what would be birthed from it.

There are moments in life when you know there is something somewhere out there for you on a level better or higher than where you are. You don't know exactly what it is or how to get there, but you have to get there! You may be seeking God for the path, and you're waiting to hear from Him to direct you.

Or perhaps, you've heard from Him. You've done just what He told you to do. Yet, there is no bloom from the ground you have broken, the seeds you've sown, the fertilizer you added, and the daily watering, and you are like me, a lady in waiting. If you feel this way, this word is for you.

Esther, an orphan raised by her cousin Mordecai as a Jewish girl in a Persian land, is our lady in waiting in this text. She was snatched from the safety of her adoptive father and brought to the palace to become a member of the king's harem while he was searching for a queen. One of the hundreds of girls with only one chance, one night, one moment, to win the king's favor. At this moment, she could either be another part of the harem where she would become a concubine, or she could be elevated as wife and queen of all of Persia. Chances were slim that the king would see something in her with so many beautiful women that caused her to have more favor than the rest. But this was her lot, and she waited.

The Bible says that she waited for one year. Some might look at a year of massages and skin treatments as posh living. I'm sure many girls were thrilled to live in a palace and have the luxuries afforded to them there. Yet, that was not the end of Esther's purpose, and I believe she knew that. Have you felt that everyone was looking at your life, what you have, what you have been afforded, and they deem you should have nothing to long for because it should be enough? And even though you are grateful, something inside of you tells you, "This is not the end of my purpose and who I am supposed to be and the life I am supposed to live."

Have you felt like that? I have. When I meditated on what goes on in the wait and considered Esther's wait, I realized she was in hiding. Before the King could even see her, she was hidden in the harem until it was time. Now I don't know what Esther went through spiritually, but I know that there are more than beauty treatments in our preparation. When I meditated on what goes on while in hiding, the caterpillar came to mind.

I was taught in elementary school that the caterpillar goes into the cocoon to become the butterfly, but for this devotion, I needed to know more. The caterpillar starts out as a tiny larva and eats enormous amounts of food until it becomes several times its size. Do you know what that tells me? As a lady-in-waiting, you must eat a lot of God's word. The more you eat of it, the more you grow.

Isaiah said his word is like honey from a honeycomb. Eat of its goodness and see how you grow exponentially in the wait! I learned that as it gets close to the metamorphosis, a hard substance is formed just under the top layer of the caterpillar. When the top layer is shed, the hard substance serves as the protective barrier for the inside. You don't know what is being formed on the inside while you are eating His word and communing with Him. However, some protective barriers are being put in place for you when you need them.

After so much eating and time, the caterpillar is hidden in what they now call a pupa or chrysalis. The caterpillar releases digestive enzymes that pretty much causes it to 'eat itself' and turn into this gooey substance. I thought- why would it eat itself? Why release an enzyme to break itself down??

Then I thought about my own transformations.

I am never transformed until I break all the way down before my God. God loves a broken heart and a contrite spirit. This is when He can do His best work. He wants you to be like He intended in the Garden of Eden. He wants you to be completely naked before Him. It doesn't matter how ugly or messed up you are. His strength is made perfect in your weakness. So become putty in His hands-clay for the potter and watch what masterpiece He can turn you into.

When the caterpillar is in hiding, you can't see what is going on inside. What happens in there is that it completely liquidizes into a gooey substance and then metamorphosis transpires slowly over 10 days. Somehow that gooey liquid turns into a butterfly. Something so beautiful from something so unappealing breaks forth!

Scientists still don't know how it is done. They just know that everything changes about it-how it looks, how it eats, moves, senses, and then it is in a state where it can produce. So, your lady-in waiting stage could be the feeding and growing stage or the 'hiding' stage.

If you are in the hiding stage, remain broken before Him, in the lowest state you can be, yielding yourself to Him to do the reshaping. Remain in your cocoon. Shut anything off that would dare to mess up the process, and don't burst out before time. Then, when the time has "fully come," the lady will be brought forth as a most beautiful creature for her God-given-glorifying purpose. Eat and be broken. Eat and be broken. Eat and be broken while you wait...

If you had only one moment in time to secure the elevation of your bud breaking forth into bloom, wouldn't you want to make sure that you were prepared for your moment? Would you rather have one month to learn and prepare for the comprehensive exam or the whole semester?

I want as much time as possible to ensure I have the knowledge down pat. I know that isn't what you want to hear because it isn't what I want to hear either. I want what I want right now, and it may even seem like I've been overlooked and my time is almost over, but I'm learning to take the time as a preparation time. Trust that God has you hidden right now for a reason. Trust that He is molding and shaping you, and you are in metamorphosis. You will be an entirely different creature with a whole new shape and size when you break forth.

Like Esther, you will find favor in those you come across. Most assuredly, you will find favor with the vessel God will use to elevate your position. I know it's hard. I know you're tired. I know you are ready, but trust God in your wait. Eat and be broken. In due season, you will break forth!

Let's Pray…

Father God, I come to you right now acknowledging you as The Sovereign God. You reign above heaven and earth. The earth is your footstool, and I am here to exhibit your glory. Lord, you know my desires. And you know I have asked my desires to be in line with Your will. That something on the inside of me is burning, Lord, and I believe in you for its manifestation. For whatever reason, you have chosen not to give it to me in this season, and I know you must have a rationale for it. Even though I want it now, I yield to You, for I know You have classified information. Where I am hard, stubborn, stiff-necked, and not wanting to bend, please accept me when I am broken before you as the lowest denominator of myself. I am but putty in Your hands. In Your hands is the only place I want to be, Lord. Be my potter. Remold me. Reshape me. Make me a vessel that is changed and worthy of the blessing You have for me. Prepare me for my 'break forth' moment. And Lord, in all things, let this not be just for my pleasure, but for the assigned purpose You have for me in Your Kingdom. Be with me while I am Your lady-in-waiting. In Jesus' name, I pray and thank you, God, for hearing and answering this prayer. Amen.

DEVOTION 6:LADY IN WAITING–PART II

Esther 2: 8-9, 12-18 When the king's order and edict had been proclaimed, many young women were brought to the citadel of Susa and put under the care of Hegai. Esther also was taken to the king's palace and entrusted to Hegai, who had charge of the harem. She pleased him and won his favor. Immediately he provided her with her beauty treatments and special food. He assigned to her seven female attendants selected from the king's palace and moved her and her attendants into the best place in the harem... Before a young woman's turn came to go in to King Xerxes, she had to complete twelve months of beauty treatments prescribed for the women, six months with oil of myrrh and six with perfumes and cosmetics. And this is how she would go to the king: Anything she wanted was given her to take with her from the harem to the king's palace. In the evening she would go there and in the morning return to another part of the harem to the care of Shaashgaz, the king's eunuch who was in charge of the concubines. She would not return to the king unless he was pleased with her and summoned her by name. When the turn came for Esther (the young woman Mordecai had adopted, the daughter of his uncle Abihail) to go to the king, she asked for nothing other than

what Hegai, the king's eunuch who was in charge of the harem, suggested. And Esther won the favor of everyone who saw her. She was taken to King Xerxes in the royal residence in the tenth month, the month of Tebeth, in the seventh year of his reign. Now the king was attracted to Esther more than to any of the other women, and she won his favor and approval more than any of the other virgins. So he set a royal crown on her head and made her queen instead of Vashti. And the king gave a great banquet, Esther's banquet, for all his nobles and officials. He proclaimed a holiday throughout the provinces and distributed gifts with royal liberality.
(New International Version)

I'm sure you probably gathered by now that the story of Queen Esther is one of my favorite stories in the Bible. First, we must note that even though she grew up in Persia, she was a part of the Israelite nation. The Israelites had been brought there in captivity, and her uncle Mordecai had been selected as an official at the palace. As an orphan raised by her uncle, Esther was taught the ways of the God of Abraham, despite being surrounded by pagans.

Xerxes was King of Persia at the time, and his queen, Vashti, mocked him. As a result, she was banished from her role as queen and the kingdom. A search was done for a new queen, bringing beautiful young virgins to the palace to please the king. Each woman had her chance to win the crown, and her chance centered on her one night with the king.

As mentioned in the previous devotion, it was a year-long process of skin and beauty treatments and training on how to handle yourself as a lady of the court. Then, after one night with the king, you were his and could not be given to another. You became a part of his harem, only to be used for his pleasure if he called upon you. I just can NOT imagine! A whole year of skin exfoliations, paraffin wax manicures and pedicures, shaving legs, arching eyebrows, hair treatments, special diets, etc., waiting for my chance to possibly be used once and tossed away, no adoration to be had from any other man, and perhaps not even the king if he wasn't feeling me! Well, Esther was one of these ladies in waiting.

Let's look at two things Esther did during the wait.

She was obedient to her Uncle Mordecai who raised her. One thing Mordecai told her was not to reveal her nationality, and she followed his instructions. She trusted her adopted father that provided and took care of her all her life. He was wise enough and loved her enough to instruct her in what was best for her. Do you not have a Father who does the same? Do you not have a Father who sacrificed His Son on the cross when you were orphaned and outside of the heavenly family so that you might be adopted into the family? He could have left you on the outside, but He loved you so much His Son gave His life so that your life could be lived more abundantly.

Has He not been providing for you and caring for you all your life? Even before your life began, He had you on His mind! Being the omniscient, all-knowing God, should we not trust His instructions? Surely, He has our best interests at heart. So, why ignore His instructions? Why find excuses to dismiss them? When we don't follow them, our steps are not ordered, and the path we take is on our own.

Ladies, follow the instructions from your Heavenly Father. He gives instructions in His Word and sometimes through His Holy Spirit. It may not make sense to you but follow His instructions. It is hard when you don't know the outcome but be obedient and follow His instructions.

In the Passion Translation, Proverbs 3: 5-6 reads, *"Trust the Lord completely, and do not rely on your own opinions. With all your heart, rely on him to guide you, and he will lead you in every decision you make. Become intimate with Him in whatever you do, and He will lead you wherever you go."*

Rely on the proper counsel for advice. When it was Esther's turn for the King, she could have taken anything she wanted. She probably had seen what others had taken and could have tried to outdo them. But, doing too much can be a detriment instead of a help in gaining favor.

Esther relinquished her right to choose what she wanted for her night with the King. Whatever the chamberlain Hegai suggested, she took. She was not interested in pleasing herself when it was her turn. Her desire was to please the King, and she trusted Hegai with what he would like. The Bible says that when she took what Hegai suggested, she was admired by all who saw her. I want to believe that not only was it physical, but her spiritual humility shone through as beauty that compared to none other.

During the process, be careful of the counsel you seek for advice.

When you know God has placed the proper counsel for you in your situation for this season, yield to it.

Let's Pray…

Lord God, we thank you for the process. We may not like it. We may pray that it comes to an end soon. But in the midst of the process, we ask for your guidance. While we wait, Lord, send us divinely appointed counsel. We do not want to miss or mess up any opportunity for advancement or promise, Lord. In our flesh, we will make mistakes. In doing what we think is right, we will mess up. We don't want that, Lord. So, we surrender to you. Tell us what to do and what not to do. Tell how us how to present ourselves when our opportunity comes. Let your Word be hidden in our hearts and become a part of who we are. Let our inner beauty shine where when men see us, they know that we are yours. We know the prediction of victory is sure when we follow you, Lord. Help us to be obedient, follow your instructions and only the counsel of those you have placed in our path during our wait. We give you all the praise. In the name of Jesus, we ask these things. Amen.

DEVOTION 7:AS THEY WENT

St. Luke 17:11-19 And it came to pass, as he went to Jerusalem, that he passed through the midst of Samaria and Galilee. And as he entered into a certain village, there met him ten men that were lepers, which stood afar off: And they lifted up their voices, and said, Jesus, Master, have mercy on us. And when he saw them, he said unto them, Go shew yourselves unto the priests. And it came to pass, that, as they went, they were cleansed. And one of them, when he saw that he was healed, turned back, and with a loud voice glorified God, And fell down on his face at his feet, giving him thanks: and he was a Samaritan. And Jesus answering said, Were there not ten cleansed? but where are the nine? There are not found that returned to give glory to God, save this stranger. And he said unto him, Arise, go thy way: thy faith hath made thee whole. (King James Version)

In life, we are met with challenges. There is an old church saying about storms: "Either you just got out of one, you are in one, or you are on your way to one."

Job 14 tells that man is born of a woman, his days are few, and they are full of trouble. How we react in times of crisis as a believer makes the difference. Even though I have read and heard these Bible verses many times, several things have come to my spirit that I want to share upon reflection.

In the text of this devotion, we find ten lepers. Leprosy is mentioned several times in the Bible and represents a set of contagious skin diseases. Lepers were exiled from the community and shunned. Jesus is passing through the middle of Samaria and Galilee. These ten lepers, recognizing who He is, cry out to Him.

Note that they recognize *who* He is. Whether your situation is as deplorable as our friends here or whether it is a different kind of challenge, I want to ask you, "Do you recognize *who* Jesus is?" I am not talking about what others say about Him. After knowing His track record, who do you say that He is??

I am guilty of focusing on my problem and not on the One who is the problem-solver. He is Immanuel, the God who is with us! He is El Elyon, the Most High God! He is El Roi, the God Who Sees Me! He is Jehovah Rapha, the Lord, our Healer! He is El Shaddai, The Almighty God! You need to know WHO Jesus is!

When I need judicial help, I look for one titled Attorney at Law. When I need skincare help, I look for one titled Doctor of Dermatology. When I need help with home buying, I look for one titled Mortgage Broker. But there will be times in life when things will come up that man cannot help you with. You need the one titled Jesus the Christ, the Son of the Living God. Only when you know WHO He is can you discern WHAT He can do. I feel this right here!!

Recognizing who Jesus was, the text says they met Him. They went to where Jesus was. Where can you find Jesus?

John 1 says He is the Word, so you must dig in the Word to meet Him.

Psalm 22 says that He inhabits the praises of His people. That means that He lives in, abides, or occupies the environment where His praises go forth. So, you must praise Him to inhabit the environment where He is.

Jeremiah 29 says God Himself said, "When you come and pray to me, I will listen."

There is something about getting on bended knee, shutting everyone and everything else out, and talking to Him that helps place you where He is. Word. Praise. Prayer. Word. Praise. Prayer. Get where He is and when you do, note your position.

The lepers humbly stood afar off yet unashamedly asked for what they needed. We are nothing but filthy rags before Him, and we humbly go before the Holy God. However, our position as daughters of the King and joint heirs with Christ yields us the privilege and right to cry out and ask for what we need.

Hebrews 4 reminds us that our High Priest is not out of touch with our reality. He made Himself kin to us, walking earth in the flesh, so He can empathize and feel what we are going through. It is not alien to Him. Because He did this, we can come boldly to the throne and get mercy, grace, and whatever we need!

Matthew 7 says that we, being evil, give our children good gifts. Will not our Father provide much more good gifts to us?

Sometimes when I pray, I say, "God, you said you could do exceedingly abundantly above what we could think or ask, and I know I can think up some stuff! So, show out for me!"

Know who Jesus is. Meet Him where He is. Ask for what you need. Then, walk on the Word He gives. Walking on His word is a sermon within itself.

I am reminded of Peter on the boat in the storm. He needed assurance that it was Jesus on the waves and commanded, "If it is you, Lord, bid me to come out there where you are." Jesus' Word was, "Come." It was simple. Just "come." Peter went on that Word and got out of the ship. He didn't need a life jacket, nor was he turned into a mermaid. He went on the Word of the Lord.

Many people criticize Peter for looking around at the conditions of the sea, which caused him to sink. But truth be told, we are creatures of the same habit. We will walk on the Word for a while. But, let the situation throw a curveball or continue a little longer than we expected…we, too, will move focus off the Word and sink in our fear and doubt. When Peter did sink, he had sense enough to call out to the One who could save Him. Sometimes when we doubt, we feel guilty, ashamed of our disbelief and lack of trust in God, and even get frustrated for not holding on to our faith. Do not wallow in that. Someone is allowing the Devil to hold their slips on this faith journey as a weapon to wave in their face, making you believe the promise is forfeited. That is not so, my sister.

In Mark 9, when the father of the demon-possessed child came to Jesus, He told him all things were possible to anyone who believed. With tears, the father declared, "Lord, help my unbelief!" What did Jesus do? He rebuked the unclean spirit to enter the child no more and lifted the child up.

Ask God to help your unbelief. I know that our God is merciful. He will come to your rescue. When He gives you the Word, walk on it. The lepers did. There was nothing that changed in their situation according to the text. However, they went with no inkling of when or how their prayers would be answered. But, as they went, something happened! Walking on the Word brought their miracle. They were cleansed!! The key is it happened "as they went."

I, myself, struggle with believing God for a situation that has not changed. But He keeps giving me Word that He Will turn it around!! I sink sometimes, but when I do, I have to say, "I'm sorry, Lord, for doubting you. Help my unbelief!! Your track record is impeccable! I have no reason to believe that You would do anything less than something good for me. In fact, I know of times when You moved, without me doing a thing, and turned things around to be better for me when at first it seemed as if I had lost. Lord, help me to walk until my water turns to wine! Help me to walk and praise until the cracks come into my Jericho walls. Help me tell the story of how you moved because 'I went'!"

Join me, sisters! Hold on! Don't stall! Keep moving! Keep trusting! Keep moving! Keep believing! It's going to happen 'as we go'!

Let's Pray...

Father God, I come in the name of Jesus, thanking you for being the One True God!! The Almighty God!! We know Who you are and the Power you have!! Lord, we know that you are so powerful that our blessings were framed before the world began. You were so considerate of little old us that you put just that much thought into how everything for us would play out. Father, right now, I pray for my sisters reading this. We have trials down here in this world. Sometimes, we don't see our way out. We don't know how we will make it through. Occasionally, our doubt has us looking at the situation and not the situation-changer. Lord, right now, touch my sister. Let her mind be renewed and transformed. Give her the knowledge of Your Word and will for her life. Let no false prophecies or words reign causing conflict, trouble and confusion. Let Your Word reign, God! Allow her to hear the voice of your Holy Spirit and rest in it. Let her rest in it, Lord. Rest like the dew on the morning grass. Give her spirit rest, Lord. Let her rest in that if you said it, that settles it! Give the boldness to walk on your word, KNOWING that you will perform what You said as she goes. As she goes. As she goes. We rebuke any darts thrown at her as she goes. We command all thoughts bringing doubt and confusion as she goes to go back to Hell where they come from. They must bow and be obedient to Christ. Lord, you reign, you lead, you comfort, you guide, you equip, you protect, you rest in her...as she goes. In the mighty name of Jesus, the Christ, we pray. It is so. Amen.

III

TIME

DEVOTION 8: IT'S JUST A MATTER OF TIME

Habakkuk 2:1-3 I will stand upon my watch, and set me upon the tower, and will watch to see what he will say unto me, and what I shall answer when I am reproved. And the LORD answered me, and said, Write the vision, and make it plain upon tables, that he may run that readeth it. For the vision is yet for an appointed time, but at the end it shall speak, and not lie: though it tarry, wait for it; because it will surely come, it will not tarry. (Kings James Version)

My mind has pondered over the story of Sleeping Beauty. In the story, a king and queen have a beautiful baby girl and invite all the fairies in the kingdom to the baby's celebration, except one they forgot. All the fairies profess good things over the child. Then the one they forgot shows up. The angry fairy swears that when the princess turns 16, she will injure herself with a spindle and die. The king and queen were dismayed, but one fairy left had not yet spoken anything over the baby and declared she wouldn't die, but she would fall into a very deep sleep.

At 16, despite the efforts of her parents to rid the kingdom of spindles, she haps upon one, injures herself, and falls asleep. The fairy comes to tell the queen she doesn't know how long it will be, perhaps 100 years before the girl awakens, but she indeed will wake up at an appointed time. The fairy puts the whole castle and its inhabitants to sleep, waiting for the curse to be broken. For 100 years, briars, thistles, vines, and branches grew up over the castle courtyards to form a tangled forest. Finally, a prince with a pure heart, wanders across the woods and, intrigued by it, enters to see what it holds. Almost giving up and turning back around, cutting, and breaking through the thick, tangled mess, he finds a castle with high towers. As he approaches, he thinks all the inhabitants are dead, then realizes they are just asleep. He wanders the entire castle until he comes to the princess's room, and love overcomes him. He kisses her hand, and the spell is broken. She and the rest of the castle awake. When the princess sees the prince, she declares, "Finally, you are here! I've waited so long for you in my dreams!" And, of course, they live happily ever after.

That which was spoken over the princess came to pass. It just took time. Many of us have a vision that we've held on to for so long that we are tired of waiting for it to materialize. Time just does not seem to be on our side. We ask…

- *Have I just wasted all this time believing God for this?*
- *Maybe I should just be content with what I have and where I am now.*
- *Surely, it would have happened by now if it was in His will.*
- *Maybe he's trying to show me that wasn't His plan...*

Yes, the heart is deceitful. Sometimes I have tried to make some things be God's will when it was something in **my** head and heart. All of us good church folks can take a piece of the Word and fit it to our circumstances when we want something bad enough to try to convince ourselves that what we want is His will. So, I encourage you and me to do as the prophet Habakkuk. Stand watch to see what it is **God** will say to you.

Looking at the text about Habakkuk, take note that there were several positions in the olden days that carried the role of the watchman. When it was near harvest time, watchmen were set over the fields to ensure predators and thieves didn't steal the crop. They were set to protect flocks by night and set upon city gate towers to warn of impending intrusion to the land. It is not a sedentary position at all. A watchman must be constant, looking to and fro, to defend the territory, discerning any potential threat. Habakkuk says he is set upon a tower-high, above, apart.

You must set yourself-the way you talk, walk, act, the life that you live-above the rest of the world. Why? Take note: The watchman doesn't have the answer. He's waiting to hear the answer from God. You cannot be below: mingling with the world, consorting with worldly ideas and norms, thinking you will be able to hear what God has to say to you.

Now, no one is telling you to be standoffish, or present as 'holier than thou.' Your focus time must be in prayer, study, and meditation with the Lord to get close enough to Him to hear what He has to say. Sometimes, popular TV shows, Social Media, and social gatherings must be set aside to hear clearly.

When you doubt a vision, whether it was really of God or not, don't abort it in frustration. Instead, take the time to see what He has to say about it.

It could not be of God, and the blocks you are experiencing are hidden blessings, rerouting you to your destined road.

But it could be very near harvest time, and that's why you're experiencing all the discombobulation about it that you are.

I don't care what it is. Going to school, completing a certification, opening a business, seeking a new position, hoping for a new relationship, or direction in the ministry. Seek to protect the vision of it from demonic heresies floating in your mind that will steal it from you. The thief comes to kill, steal, and destroy. But Jesus came so that we could experience more abundant life. It may not be instant, but God WILL speak.

Psalm 85:8 reads, *"I will hear what God the LORD will speak: for he will speak peace unto his people, and to his saints: but let them not turn again to folly."*

God will answer if you seek His face. And when He does answer- Write His answer concerning your vision down! You need to do it to make it clear for yourself. You need to do it so you can remember when your spirit is weak and begins to doubt. Know that His word will not return void, and no matter how long it tarries-it SHALL come to pass.

It was 25 years before Abraham's vision manifested, but IT CAME TO PASS. Four hundred years of no prophecies for

Israel, but what Isaiah, Micah, and Jeremiah declared about the Messiah, the Christ Child, IT CAME TO PASS. The Lord WILL perfect that concerning you! Sooner or later, know that it WILL happen for you at that APPOINTED TIME. It WILL happen for me.

I've heard so many times: The wait is for you, so you can be prepared. And sometimes, that is true. But I've also heard: The wait is for the other participants in the vision. They aren't ready yet. You don't want a cake out of the oven before time-it will still be runny on the inside! And sometimes, that is true, too.

But sometimes: The wait ain't even got nothing to do with you! It's about HIM! Look at Lazarus…dead for 4 days…it was so that God might get the glory! It was necessary to make sure he was good and dead for people to believe that Jesus had the power to resurrect. God may be using you and your situation to be one of His "Can't Be Nobody But God" testimonies. Trust in Him. Hold out. No matter what demonic fairy Satan has set loose to curse you, if MY GOD wills a thing, it's GOT to come to pass. At His Appointed Time. Just start speaking, "And it came to pass" over your situation because in God's eternal realm, it already is!! Ha! For us in the earth realm, it's just a matter of time.

And it came to pass…And it came to pass…And it came to pass…

Let's Pray…

Lord, I come ready to take my station on the tower. I am ready to stand to see what You have to say to me. I don't want my heart to get sick wishing for something not in Your will. I want to know your will, and I need you to tell me. I need to hear a word from you. Erase anything I put with my tongue in the atmosphere that is not backed by Your word. You tell me what to say, and I will say it. You tell me what to declare, and I will declare it. As I sacrifice and separate myself from things that might distract me, speak to me clearly and let your Holy Spirit guide me as I write the vision. Not my vision, but Yours, Lord. For I know that Your Word is true. I know that Your word shall not return void. If I stand on Your word and Your vision, I don't have to worry about any contingencies. I know that heaven and earth will pass away before Your word fails. Let Your word for my life be a lamp unto my feet and a light unto my path. Even when the day is lonely, I will wait until my change comes. Even when the day is long, I will wait until my change comes. God, what you have for me is for me, and it SHALL come to pass. Speak to me. Reassure me. Confirm for me. Help me stand on Your promise, and I will be careful to give You all praise, glory, and honor. In the mighty name of Jesus, we do ask these things. Amen and thank God.

DEVOTION 9:AFTER THIS

Genesis 18: 1-14; 21: 1-2 The LORD appeared to Abraham near the great trees of Mamre while he was sitting at the entrance to his tent in the heat of the day. Abraham looked up and saw three men standing nearby. When he saw them, he hurried from the entrance of his tent to meet them and bowed low to the ground. He said, "If I have found favor in your eyes, my lord, do not pass your servant by. Let a little water be brought, and then you may all wash your feet and rest under this tree. Let me get you something to eat, so you can be refreshed and then go on your way—now that you have come to your servant." "Very well," they answered, "do as you say." So Abraham hurried into the tent to Sarah. "Quick," he said, "get three seahs of the finest flour and knead it and bake some bread." Then he ran to the herd and selected a choice, tender calf and gave it to a servant, who hurried to prepare it. He then brought some curds and milk and the calf that had been prepared, and set these before them. While they ate, he stood near them under a tree. "Where is your wife Sarah?" they asked him. "There, in the tent," he said. Then one of them said, "I will surely return to you about this time next year, and Sarah your wife will have a son." Now Sarah was listening at the entrance to the tent, which was behind him. Abraham and

Sarah were already very old, and Sarah was past the age of childbearing. So Sarah laughed to herself as she thought, "After I am worn out and my lord is old, will I now have this pleasure?" Then the LORD said to Abraham, "Why did Sarah laugh and say, 'Will I really have a child, now that I am old?' Is anything too hard for the LORD? I will return to you at the appointed time next year, and Sarah will have a son… Now the Lord was gracious to Sarah as he had said, and the Lord did for Sarah what he had promised. Sarah became pregnant and bore a son to Abraham in his old age, at the very time God had promised him. (New International Version)

What do we know about Sarah? We know her as Abraham's wife. We know that she must've been beautiful because kings wanted her. She had a husband. A wealthy and prosperous husband. She had servants. She had all the amenities of life she needed and more. And she had a promise…

Yes, she had a promise. But at the point of this text, the promise probably did not mean anything to her. Let's revisit Sarah's history. God had promised that Abraham would be the father of many nations. As long as Sarah had waited for God to come through on His promise, it never happened. After about 13 years of waiting on it, she decided to take matters into her own hand and give Abraham her handmaid Hagar, who had Ishmael. That was a complete disaster. The woman taunted Sarah so that Sarah used her authority to make Hagar's life hell. She was so mean to the woman that Hagar fled from Sarah's house.

I know many people have thought–Now, Sarah, you were wrong for that. You were the one who told her to go with your husband in the first place, and then you're gonna have a problem with it? Girl, please. That's what you get for digging into God's business.

But I can't be so quick to reprimand Sarah, for I have gotten tired of waiting on God and tried to make things be something they were not supposed to be myself. Have you never gotten involved with someone or something that you know was beneath the promise of God, but because of the void you felt, you took what you had in front of you and tried to make do? You figure God can bless you with the scraps you have since He hasn't moved to do it the way you thought He was going to. You have done it, and I have done it, too. Then when the consequences of our actions yield strife, we get mad at ourselves for putting our hands into it.

So what do you do when you've put your hands into it, the mess is made, and you're still without what God promised you?? If you're like me, you may gather in your mind that because of your mess, God reneges on His promise, and you will not see it in your lifetime. So, you become content with the good things you have and suppose that you have forfeited your chance at what you have longed for. Well, maybe not all the way content. Perhaps you accept going through the motions of life without the promise. I'm sure you beat yourself up about it sometimes. But then sometimes you look at people (who you see to be worse than you) that get to receive the same promise and wonder-Why does God hate me so that He overlooks them and their faults and gives them the gift, but because I messed up, He wants to treat me like a stepchild?

Yes, I said it. You feel as if God does not love you the way He loves others because if He did, He wouldn't put you through the torture of promising you something, getting you excited about the vision of the promise, and allowing your heart and spirit to anticipate the promise, only to be let down. It's like the fable of the fox with the grapes in a vine so high that when he couldn't reach them, he tells himself they weren't good anyway.

That is what Satan will do to us, y'all. He will sow seeds of doubt, frustration, jealousy, bitterness, and anger that will sprout weeds to choke the life out of that part of our spirit that believes God for the promise.

But there is something I want you to know.

In Hebrews 11, it says that the ages were framed by Him. I said "'Ages'"-that means times past, times present, and times to come-have already been framed by Him. If it's framed, it's set. There's no changing it. He doesn't have to figure out how He will make anything come to pass. He's already set just how it's going to play out. We may not know the ins and outs, but He does. He knows the ins and outs of your situation the same way He did about Sarah's.

If God gave you a word and it seems that time has passed for it to come to fruition, ask yourself this. Is anything too hard for God? Is it something impossible for Him to do? God has not forgotten about what He said to you. Sometimes our God likes dramatic entrances. Sometimes our God desires to be fashionably late. Sometimes our God wants you and your audience to say, "You mean to tell me that after this…He's gonna do it?"

Really??? After this??? After all this time! After all money is gone. After you've been made a fool of. After you lost your job. After the contract didn't go through. After you got looked over, picked over, and ran over. After you've thrown everybody else a baby shower. After you've been a bridesmaid in everybody else's wedding. After everyone else in your family and circle has bypassed you with degrees. After you've celebrated their graduations. After years and even decades, those who used to cheer you on have silenced their chants and faded into the background because they, too, feel like God must not be planning to come through for you. After family and your loved ones want you to give it up, too, because it hurts them to see you hurt. Hurt that God has forgotten about it or His answer is no. After no one believes anymore but you! After you have fought like hell to make yourself keep believing, and it's not healthy to hold on anymore to this notion, so you decide to set it down.

AFTER THIS!!! After this, God will bring you a Ramah word. A word to remind you of what He said. And when He does, you better reach down to that dry bone inside your spirit. Yield it to the Holy Ghost so that He can breathe on it and resurrect your faith and mind to get ready because He's coming with His promise…after this.

Hannah was looking like a drunk woman praying in church, but God sent her a 'word by the priest'…but it was only in her 'after this.'

The Canaanite woman needed help for her child, left her child with someone else, and made the trip to Jesus. When she gets there, she is dissed by the disciples. Even Jesus called her a dog, yet He gave her a 'request granted' word…but it was only in her 'after this.'

Lazarus had been dead for 4 long days, and Martha knew the situation was a stinky one. Yet, Jesus had a 'come forth' word… but it was only in their 'after this.'

Jesus, Himself, had been ostracized, criticized, abandoned by loved ones, beaten, bled, and hung on a cross. He had asked His Father in the Garden of Gethsemane if He could bypass that bitter cup but yielded when He said, "Nevertheless, not my will. Let your will be done."

Having never been separated from His father, He cried out, "Eli, Eli, lama sabachthani" – "My God! My God! Why have you forsaken for me?" Even though He was so close to the end, I believe He held on to His own word where He said, "Destroy this temple. But in three days, I will raise it up." Internally, He had a 'raise it up word'…but it could only be manifested 'after this.'

Sometimes we make ourselves believe what we want is God's will, and it is not. He does not have to come through on what we say. But He HAS to come through on HE SAYS!!! So, if He comes back around with a word to confirm His promise, and it's at a time too ludicrous to believe it, I'm talking about a clock has struck 12 and the ball is over kinda time, you better raise up and say…Wait a minute!!! Look at my God! He's chosen me for an 'After This' kinda miracle!!! Get ready! Get ready! Get ready for your promise! It is coming…after this…

Let's Pray...

Spirit of the Living God, I come to You right now in humility, yet in confidence. Not in the confidence of my might but in the faith of who You are. Someone has said that You are the God of miracles, signs, and wonders. I'm believing you to be a wonder-working God for me right now in my situation. Time and circumstance would lead me to conclude that my miracle is nothing but just my imagination running away with me. However, that is not what I BELIEVE. I BELIEVE in the power of the risen Savior, my Redeemer, my Deliverer, who sits at the right of God and is my Advocate. Jesus, I call on Your name right now. I call on the name with power to break chains. Healing power. Resurrecting power. Wonder-working power. For man, it may be too late. But for You, the time is just right. I call on You to show Yourself El-Shaddai, the Almighty God, in my After This. Only You and I know the ins and outs, the breaking, the molding, the breaking, the remolding, the hurt, the heartbreak, the tears that have been shed. The hope that would be lost but has been stirred up again. Only You and I know how I have held on to my faith that there will be glory After This. I call on You to turn things around. I call on You to bring me out. I call on You to vindicate me. I call on You to give me joy for my sorrow. I call on You to manifest what you set in the spiritual realm in the natural realm. I call on You to help me hold on until the day that you set as the appointed time...to hold on and don't let go of my faith...my faith for After This. Anoint me afresh so that your mercy, grace, and favor will reign on me at that specified time. Your presence will overshadow me, and I, too, will be able to sing praises and tell of Your glory in my After This. I declare and decree it to be done by faith in the mighty name of Jesus the Christ. Amen.

IV

GOD AS

DEVOTION 10:GOD AS PROTECTOR: HE IS FOR ME

Psalm 55:18 With his peace, he will rescue my soul from the war raged against me, because there are many soldiers fighting against me.
(God's Word Translation)

Have you ever felt like you were meant to be somewhere different than the place in life you are at present? Then, once you started to accept that you were internally more than who you presently were exhibiting, you started getting attack after attack? As I write this book, I can tell you that I know God called me as an anointed woman of God and that His plan for me and my ministry is not limited to the zone I've created for myself. My destiny is higher than what I imagine. It has been confirmed by the many attacks Satan has placed in my way since grasping hold of my calling. If you are like me, these attacks may distract you from remembering who you have fighting on your side. It is easy to get bogged down in how many are fighting against you. But you must keep in mind that you have an ultimate protector, and He is for you.

Making mention of Dorothy from the Wizard of Oz, we know

that walking around as a citizen of Oz was not the destination of her calling. She was not destined to be a citizen of Oz. The place she was trying to get to was back home in Kansas. However, in that story, she was called to be waaay more than a little girl with a dog named Toto on a farm with Auntie Em. Dorothy had a work to do in the land of Oz. Unfortunately, the Wicked Witch of the West was working to keep her from doing it. One thing the Wicked Witch couldn't touch, though, was the red shoes Dorothy had with remarkable power. She couldn't touch them unless Dorothy was defeated because of a magical barrier the shoes had attached to the owner.

She sent so many things Dorothy's way to distract her from her destiny. In the book version, for a little human girl, the Witch used a pack of wolves, a flock of crows, a spell from a deadly poppy field, and a group of Winkie slaves to fight her. When all that didn't work, she sent her flying monkeys, but it was all to no avail. Not even knowing her power over the witch, Dorothy throws a bucket of water on her and completes her designated task in Oz-killing the Witch.

The Winkies, flying monkeys, and all are then free, which was a part of the work Dorothy was sent to Oz to do. Dorothy really had no desire to even fool around with this witch. She just wanted the comfort of Kansas. She didn't even take note that she had already killed the sister witch, and it was given to her to kill the other one, too, to help free other creatures in the land.

God has given you work to do in His kingdom, and it doesn't come with what's always familiar and comfortable for you. You probably have no desire to even fool with some of the territories you've been called to but look back over your life. Without even knowing it, God has given you the power to kill Satan's plan...that job that you took or didn't take...that relationship you didn't get too deep in... that financial venture that you didn't take up.

Now that you look back, you can see God has protected you from some things that would have hindered you from being as far along as you are now. I know I can definitely praise Him for that! Can you not look back and see that He was for you in past battles?

As far as the attacks go-even though it is hell to endure them-He has a barrier, a hedge of protection, around you. God knows you have something mighty for the Kingdom, and He will not let anything Satan throws your way prosper. And you better believe Satan has some demons to throw at you!

Looking at Mark 5, we are told of a man possessed by demons coming out of the tombs to meet Jesus. When asked what his name was, he says, "Legion, for we are many." Merriam-Webster describes the term legion as: A large group of soldiers; the principal unit of the Roman army comprising 3,000-6,000-foot soldiers with calvary; a large military force.

Why was it necessary for the Devil to invest so much against this one man? In a sermon once, Bishop T. D. Jakes of the Potter's House said that it's because of what the man had to do for the kingdom. In the 20th verse of Mark 5, it tells us how the man began to proclaim in the city of the great things Jesus had done for him and how ALL men did marvel. This man was going to reach too many people and bring too much acclaim to the cause of Christ for Satan not to oppose it.

Likewise, Sis, there are some people you must reach. Someone's healing, eye-opening, deliverance, conviction, or conversion may be connected to your plight in the kingdom. You may feel a war raging against you and demons as soldiers fighting you at every turn. But thank God for His peace that He will give in the midst of it all. He will rescue the turmoil in your soul and give you what you need to answer His call.

How was Moses able to tell Pharoah that he had to let the children of Israel go? Moses knew God was for him. How could Gideon take 300 men and slay 135,000 warring against him? Gideon knew God was for him. How was Joshua able to defeat the fortified city of Jericho? Joshua knew God was for him. You need to know like these warriors knew.

You have much more than Dorothy's red slippers to help you. You have a God called El Shaddai, the Almighty God! It does not matter what weapons form against you. They will not prosper! When you are His, He is on your side.

Psalm 24:8 tells you that the King of Glory is the Lord strong and mighty, and He is mighty in battle. Who can fight against Him and win? Nobody. I mean-not Nobody!! Do you remember when we were younger, playing games outside? When it was time to pick teams, we would like the best players to be on our team to ensure a win. You have the Ultimate Player! The Ultimate Warrior! The Ultimate Protector! And when you gave Him your life, He took a permanent role on your team.

That means you are destined to win! So, forget about the darts thrown at you, girl. Allow your soul to rest in the peace that He is *for you.*

Let's pray...

O Father, I thank you for being a gracious God! Forgive me for fretting and doubting outcomes when I have you on my side. I know that you understand temptation, for you went through it in the wilderness. I know that you understand inner turmoil, for you experienced it in Gethsemane. But you were victorious over it all, and so shall I be, too! When I get frustrated about continuous attacks against me while I'm doing your will, help me to remember Romans 8:31. God, if you be for me, who can be against me? I'm going to say it again. God, if you be for me, who can be against me? You are my keeper, the shade on my right hand! Rescue my soul, Lord, from anything fighting against me and my purpose. Give me your peace, Lord, like this verse the hymnist wrote: "When peace, like a river, attends all my way, when sorrows like sea billows roll, whatever my path, you have taught me to say, 'It is well; it is well with my soul.'" Thank you, God, for being my protector! Thank you, God, for securing me! I will rest in you and the protection you provide, giving you all praise, glory, and honor! I love you, Lord, and I pray this in the omnipotent name of Jesus the Christ. Amen. **Reference:** *When peace like a river (it is well ...)- Music Ministry. https://www.musicministry.org/hymns/when-peace-like-a-river-it-is-well/*

DEVOTION 11:GOD AS GOD OF THE MISFITS: THE MISFIT FITS!

Acts 9:10-15 And there was a certain disciple at Damascus, named Ananias; and to him said the Lord in a vision, Ananias. And he said, Behold, I am here, Lord. And the Lord said unto him, Arise, and go into the street which is called Straight, and enquire in the house of Judas for one called Saul, of Tarsus: for, behold, he prayeth, And hath seen in a vision a man named Ananias coming in, and putting his hand on him, that he might receive his sight. Then Ananias answered, Lord, I have heard by many of this man, how much evil he hath done to thy saints at Jerusalem: and here he hath authority from the chief priests to bind all that call on thy name. But the Lord said unto him, Go thy way: for he is a chosen vessel unto me, to bear my name before the Gentiles, and kings, and the children of Israel: (King James Version)

Often in the Christmas season, I am reminded of the movie "Rudolph and the Island of Misfit Toys." A misfit is a person who is different from other people and does not seem to belong in a particular group or situation. The toys on the island had characteristics about themselves that made them "unworthy" toys to be played with. There was a "Charlie" in the box instead of a "Jack," a train with square wheels instead of round ones, an airplane that could not fly, a bird that swims instead of flying, a cowboy riding an ostrich, and a polka-dotted elephant. Some are misfits by look, by name, by ability, or disability-a lot of possible reasons why some people are possibly deemed misfits today. However, that is not exactly why I feel like I am a misfit.

It is not my look, name, or ability/disability that has me feeling unworthy right now, but it is due to my own actions that I have deemed myself a misfit. Sometimes in life, we fall short. We make promises to God, and we only halfheartedly keep them. It's not that we are new converts and have the excuses that we are new to this thing. When we fall short, we often say, "I made a mistake…It just happened…I was gonna do it, but I forgot. Time just got away from me…" But the truth is none of these excuses are valid.

We made a *choice*…a choice to do, or not do, whatever it was. And with every choice you make, there are consequences. You had a choice to give to God first and go lacking somewhere else, and you chose to lack on God. You made a choice to entertain the conversation of that person that led you to do way more than converse with them. It didn't just happen. It was your choice to go there. You chose not to wake up early, take your lunch break, or spend 20 minutes in the bathroom just talking to God, reading His Word, meditating, or seeking Him. You choose to sleep, keep it moving with your many daily activities, or talk on the phone. It is your choice.

I made a choice to fill my head with imaginations and things that have nothing to do with me and my call. I just didn't feel like doing it – seeking God first. I wanted to do other things, so I set things concerning my call aside. I had ambition in activities I liked to do and wanted to do, but I was lacking in what God had set out for me to do. And now, where I should have been way farther along than I am, I am in a pit of dismay, feeling like a misfit. Unworthy to complete what I started. Unfit to continue in the acceptance of my call because of how so very short I fall. I am a misfit because of my own doing. Have you ever felt this way? It is not a good feeling when you are climbing higher but allow yourself to get sidetracked, and you just don't know where to go from here.

I am reminded of Saul in the 9th chapter of Acts again. Saul was ambitious in his own thing-his religion. Even though Saul was doing his own thing, God took the time to knock him off his beast and get him on the right track. Ananias was told by God to take him in, lay hands on him, and pray for him.

Ananias said, "Wait a minute! Are you talking about the Saul of Tarsus that I know? He's not a Christian. He's not one of us. He doesn't attend our church meetings. In fact, he's quite the opposite. He's the epitome of a misfit for our group! Are you sure that is who you are talking about?"

God said, "He may be a misfit to you, but I use who I want to use. And trust me, I, who scooped out the mountains and pressed down the valleys - I can take a misfit and make him fit. I have predestined him for my purpose despite his misfit ways. He is a chosen vessel unto me, and He will bear my name before Gentiles and kings and the children of Israel."

I thank God for His word and His reminding me of His word! Yes, I am still unworthy, but He who has begun this work in me will bring it to completion on the day of Jesus Christ. Do you know what that means? God is not through with me yet!

Satan **DOES NOT** have the power to use the cancerous spots of sin in my life to keep me exiled on the misfit island, away from being used by Him. Why? Because of the blood! The blood of Jesus…whew! It covers me and washes away all evidence of abnormal mutations in my body! Oh, it cleanses me! Makes me whole again! Makes me fit! It is in my weakness that I see who He really is! He is my Redeemer! Whew! Jesus' precious blood reaches and yanks me back in when I fall by the wayside!

In a misfit moment, King David said in Psalm 51, "Purge me with hyssop, and I shall be clean. Wash me, and I shall be whiter than snow." Hyssop was a plant with medicinal properties known to have virtue as an antiseptic, a cough reliever, and an expectorant. Acting as an expectorant would purge the body or clear it of something unwanted and unclean. Jesus will purify you and make you clean inside when you are under His blood.

David was an adulterer, schemer, and killer, but God made the misfit fit. Ruth was a Moabitess, a non-Israelite woman who came from serving idol gods and an outsider in Bethlehem, but God made the misfit fit. Rahab was also an outsider, not just as a woman from Jericho, but a prostitute at that. God took her, the misfit, and made her fit. In fact, the two misfits, Ruth and Rahab, are placed in the genealogy of Jesus Christ.

Amos said, "I wasn't a prophet nor the son of a prophet, but I was a herdsman and gatherer of sycamore fruit. While I was following the flock, the Lord called me and told me to prophesy unto His people Israel." Don't you see how he takes misfits and uses them for His purpose and will? Regardless of how bad the credit of your character and walk with Him is, you don't need a cosigner for the contract. Walk in what He has called you to do, who He has called you to be, and let Him perfect that which concerns you. I promise He will make you fit!

Let's pray...

Father God, I come now acknowledging you as Sovereign. You reign over everything, Lord. I bow humbly before you and your majestic ways. I am in awe of how you have considered little old me –filthy, unworthy, completely messed up. You considered me, Lord, and still thought I was worth saving and sacrificed your life for me. Please clean me up, God. Purge me with hyssop. Remove all sediments of anything not like you so that my heart may be pure before you. Remove any fragments of anything not like you from my mind and transform me by renewing my mind, Lord. You are the potter, and I am genuinely nothing but clay. Mold me and make me fit where you have called me to serve, Lord. I know I am nothing without you. I need you, Jesus, to lay your hands on me. While you are working on my mind, help me rest in the revelation that though I am unworthy, your blood has made me worthy. Your blood and its redemptive power have more than settled where I fall short. Help me to rest in being a part of your family, Lord. Help me to rest in being a recipient of the Abrahamic covenant. Help me to rest in that I am part of a royal priesthood. Help me rest in the knowledge that your coming was not in vain, and it warrants me access to experience exceedingly abundantly above what I can think or ask. Help me rest in the beauty of you taking me, a misfit, and making me fit for the purpose of your kingdom. I will be careful to give you all the praise, glory, and honor, Lord. In the mighty name of Jesus, I pray. Amen.

DEVOTION 11:GOD AS GOD OF THE MISFITS: THE MISFIT FITS!

purpose of your kingdom. I will be careful to give you all the praise, glory, and honor, Lord. In the mighty name of Jesus, I pray. Amen.

73

DEVOTION 12:GOD AS KEEPER: OH TO BE KEPT

Psalm 121:5 The LORD is thy keeper: the LORD is thy shade upon thy right hand. (King James Version)

Joshua 2: 1-24 And it was told the king of Jericho, saying, Behold, there came men in hither to night of the children of Israel to search out the country. And the king of Jericho sent unto Rahab, saying, Bring forth the men that are come to thee, which are entered into thine house: for they be come to search out all the country. And the woman took the two men, and hid them, and said thus, There came men unto me, but I wist not whence they were: And it came to pass about the time of shutting of the gate, when it was dark, that the men went out: whither the men went I wot not: pursue after them quickly; for ye shall overtake them. But she had brought them up to the roof of the house, and hid them with the stalks of flax, which she had laid in order upon the roof. And the men pursued after them the way to Jordan unto the fords: and as soon as they which pursued after them were gone out, they shut the gate. And before they were laid down, she came up unto them upon the roof; And she said unto the men, I know that the LORD hath given you the land, and that your terror is fallen upon us, and that all the inhabitants of the land faint because of you. For we have heard how the LORD dried up the water of the Red sea for you, when ye came out of Egypt; and what ye did unto the two kings of the Amorites, that were on the other side Jordan, Sihon and Og, whom ye utterly destroyed. And as soon as we had heard these things, our hearts did melt, neither did there remain any more courage in any man, because of you: for the LORD your God, he is God in heaven above, and in earth beneath. Now therefore, I pray you, swear unto me by the LORD, since I have shewed you kindness, that ye will also shew kindness unto my father's house, and give me a true token: And that ye will save alive my father, and my mother, and my brethren, and my sisters, and all that they have, and deliver our lives from death. And the men answered her, Our life for yours, if ye utter not this our business. And it shall be, when the LORD hath given us the land, that we will deal kindly and truly with thee. Then she let them down by a cord through the window: for her house was upon the town wall, and she dwelt upon the wall. And she said unto them, Get you to the mountain, lest the pursuers meet you; and hide yourselves there three days, until the pursuers be returned: and afterward may ye go your way. And the men said unto her, We will be blameless of this thine oath which thou hast made us swear. Behold, when we come into the land, thou shalt bind this line of scarlet thread in the window which thou didst let us down by: and thou shalt bring thy father, and thy mother, and thy brethren, and all thy father's household, home unto thee. And it shall be, that whosoever shall go out of the doors of thy house into the street, his blood shall be upon his head, and we will be guiltless: and whosoever shall be with thee in the house, his blood shall be on our head, if any hand be

upon him. And if thou utter this our business, then we will be quit of thine oath which thou hast made us to swear. And she said, According unto your words, so be it. And she sent them away, and they departed: and she bound the scarlet line in the window. And they went, and came unto the mountain, and abode there three days, until the pursuers were returned: and the pursuers sought them throughout all the way, but found them not. So the two men returned, and descended from the mountain, and passed over, and came to Joshua the son of Nun, and told him all things that befell them: And they said unto Joshua, Truly the LORD hath delivered into our hands all the land; for even all the inhabitants of the country do faint because of us.
(King James Version)

Joshua 6:25 And Joshua saved Rahab the harlot alive, and her father's household, and all that she had; and she dwelleth in Israel even unto this day; because she hid the messengers, which Joshua sent to spy out Jericho. (King James Version)

Ok, I know I had a lot of scriptures, but I really wanted the story of Rahab to unfold. Rahab was an innkeeper that supposedly was a harlot. Somehow, Israelite spies ended up in her home while seeking information regarding a battle strategy plan to take back to Joshua and the camp. Rahab made it known to the spies that Jericho citizens had heard of their God. Not only had they heard of Him, but they feared Him. She openly admitted that she knew their God was The One True God. She had helped the children of God by hiding them and she asked for a favor in return.

She said, "Please save my mother and father, and all my family. Promise me that you will keep us safe, for I know God has given the city to you." The spies promised that the red cord in the window would be a sign for the Israelite army not to touch them but to keep them safe. When she confessed belief in who God was and what He could do, God set in motion to move on her behalf.

Just like God kept Rahab, God will keep you! You must do like Rahab and Speak the Word! Acknowledge who He is and what He can do and watch how He works things out! I learned from a friend of mine to take Psalm 91, speak His word, and make it personal. Put your name in it: ___________ dwelleth in the secret place of the Most High and abides under the shadow of the Almighty. ___________ will say of the Lord, "He is my refuge, my God; in Him will I trust." Surely, He shall deliver _______ from the snare of the fowler and from the noisome pestilence. He shall cover ________ with His feathers and under His wings shall __________ trust...A thousand shall fall at _________'s side and ten thousand at her right hand, but it will not come nigh her...

When you speak the wondrous works of God and make it personal, God will move on your behalf. Rahab heard about the things God had done and recounted it. She said, "We know about what happened down at the Red Sea. We know about those two Amorite kings, Sihon and Og." Rahab didn't have the luxury of the written word. But we do! Go in the Word of God and recount what He has done. If He did it before, He can do it again!

In Matthew 10, Jesus said that not one sparrow will fall to the ground without the Father knowing about it. We are way more than sparrows to Him! He knows the most excruciatingly minute details of you, even to the number of hairs on your head. You better **KNOW** that God is keeping you!

One thing that I want you to consider is this: it is **four** chapters later before we see the fullness of Rahab's promise come to fruition. Rahab had done right by the men of God; she had to sit still, follow the instructions, and trust that the God of the Israelites would keep her. The Merriam-Webster dictionary says that keeping means preserving, maintaining, and supporting. She knew without God this battle and chaos would be impossible to overcome.

Somebody needs to hear this. It may look impossible-the odds stacked against you in whatever you are facing. But I want you to sit still and follow God's instructions. Trust that He will keep you! Do right by God and His people and watch how God shows up! I believe He is going to show up for me just like He promised!

In the story, the men had to go in hiding for three days, make the journey back to Joshua, issue the news, and then had to sanctify themselves. Then, they had to march to Jericho, march around Jericho, and they had to do it for 7 days before the story comes to this turning point for Rahab. And you know what? Rahab knew NOTHING, ABSOLUTELY NOTHING, about what was going on with the Israelites, their preparation, and getting ready to hold up their side of the bargain.

Sometimes God is going to tell you ABSOLUTELY NOTHING about what He is doing to set up things for you. But you have to BELIEVE and not lean to your own understanding. That is what faith is. Believing that He has you even when you cannot see it and don't know how He will do it. If you have to know all the details, it is not faith. Without faith it is impossible to please Him. I spoke of Mary in another devotion. Luke 1 states that she was blessed because of her faith. She believed that the Lord would keep and fulfill His promises to her. Oh, to be kept!

Do you know what I like most about this story? I was about to call this 'four-chapter later mark', this point in the story where Rahab is saved , the climax point. However, while writing the paragraph above, I realized it was not a climax point, just a turning point. Let me say that again. It was good, but it was not a **climax point, just a turning point**. She hadn't hit her climax mark yet, which meant the best for her was yet to come! Hundreds of years later, Matthew mentions that Rahab married Salmon and gave birth to Boaz–Yes, THE BOAZ-who married Ruth and whose seed our blessed Lord and Savior came through! Then the author of Hebrews in the 11th chapter mentions her and her faith as the reason she did not perish at Jericho. Oh, to be kept!

Her works are mentioned in the book of James, too. What will they say about you? What story will you leave? I pray that you and I both will not depend on ourselves or on man, but in the Living God – the shade on our right hand, the Rock of Ages, the strong tower. I pray we will be able to sing how wonderful it is to be kept by God!

Let's pray...

Spirit of the Living God, fall fresh on us right now! Allow us to rest in your power. Allow us to rest in your faithfulness. Allow us to be at peace even when we don't know how you are going to bring us through. Allow the Holy Spirit to bring back to our remembrance your Word. Allow us to meditate on how you kept the believers of old and help us to recount it. Allow the Holy Spirit to bring back to our remembrance how you have moved in our lives before and help us to recite it. Bring to our minds how you moved for those around us, Lord. Help us rest in this: if you did it before, you can do it again! Help us to rest comfortably in the fact that we have the most excellent insurance plan with you. No matter what accident, trouble, or mishap comes our way, we have a claims specialist that will not only restore anything lost but will issue upgrades. Our claim specialist wrote in the plan, "I come that you might have life and have it more abundantly." Rock of Ages, help us to hide in you! Help us to lean on you and rest in you! Help us to quit fretting and worrying because we are not alone. We have a keeper in you, Jesus Christ! Help us to be confident that we will sing, "Oh to be Kept by Jesus", and give you all praise, glory, and honor. These things we ask in the mighty name of Jesus. Amen!

DEVOTION 13:GOD AS GOD OF THE IMPOSSIBLE: MISSION IMPOSSIBLE

Luke 1:26-38 And in the sixth month the angel Gabriel was sent from God unto a city of Galilee, named Nazareth, to a virgin espoused to a man whose name was Joseph, of the house of David; and the virgin's name was Mary. And the angel came in unto her, and said, Hail, thou that art highly favoured, the Lord is with thee: blessed art thou among women. And when she saw him, she was troubled at his saying, and cast in her mind what manner of salutation this should be. And the angel said unto her, Fear not, Mary: for thou hast found favour with God. And, behold, thou shalt conceive in thy womb, and bring forth a son, and shalt call his name JESUS. He shall be great, and shall be called the Son of the Highest: and the Lord God shall give unto him the throne of his father David: And he shall reign over the house of Jacob for ever; and of his kingdom there shall be no end. Then said Mary unto the angel, How shall this be, seeing I know not a man? And the angel answered and said unto her, The Holy Ghost shall come upon thee, and the power of the Highest shall overshadow thee: therefore also that holy thing which shall be born of thee shall

be called the Son of God. And, behold, thy cousin Elisabeth, she hath also conceived a son in her old age: and this is the sixth month with her, who was called barren. For with God nothing shall be impossible. And Mary said, Behold the handmaid of the Lord; be it unto me according to thy word. And the angel departed from her. (King James Version)

Whether you actually watched it or not, most of us think of Tom Cruise and the mega-dollar movie series when we hear the words "Mission Impossible." Special agents, spies, high action, mysterious danger, and missions to overthrow some villain are the main plots for each movie in the series. However, I am not speaking of Tom Cruise. I am speaking of me, and I am speaking of you when I talk about Mission Impossible.

I have said before that I am in a torrential fight of faith while writing this book. What God has shown me and I what I see before me are at complete odds with one another. I have been wrong in what I believed was God before, but I know I am hearing from Him this time. I have shared this with a few of my friends. Each one of them have expressed that what I'm looking for will not happen. They are trying to get my mind to turn in another direction.

The fight is hard enough for me to walk it out in faith. Having people beside me pushing me to get off this road is making it even more difficult. I have cut off conversation with them about what God is showing me. I have learned not to be angry or upset with them about it. God did not give this for them to carry. He gave it to me.

I watched a sermon video of Minister Joyce Meyer's. She had several pregnant women come on stage in various months of the gestation period. She went to the first woman and asked, "Are you pregnant?" The woman answered, "Yes." This woman was only 6-8 weeks pregnant at the time. Joyce conveyed how she didn't look pregnant at all to them and asked, "Do you feel pregnant?"

The woman said that she did. She knew that her body was changing, and she was feeling morning sickness and more. Joyce and the audience could not outwardly tell that she was pregnant, nor could they feel that she was pregnant. But she was. She was in a stage of pregnancy where she had the revelation, but it had not been revealed yet to the outside world.

That is precisely the stage of pregnancy I am in with my dream that I am fighting for. Unfortunately, to everyone connected to me, my dream is Mission Impossible. Even the one close friend, who I thought was going to stand in agreement with me 'til the end, has left me to stand alone. But I know who can make the impossible possible. And I draw from **Luke 1** as my spiritual base for this devotion.

Young Mary was minding her own business when the angel told her she would be carrying the Christ Child. Mary was not even married yet. Mary had not even sexually been with a man yet. Her wedding date must not have been close, or else she would have thought it would happen with her and Joseph on their soon wedding night.

She asked, "How can this be and I don't even know a man?"

Gabriel revealed to her that the Holy Ghost would overshadow her, and it would happen. The scripture tells us after the first question was answered, Mary did not ask any more. She replied, "Be it unto me according to Thy word."

She did not have to know precisely what the overshadowing of the Holy Ghost entailed. She did not have to know when He would come on her – Thursday, Friday, or the 15th of the month. She did not have to know how long the process would take. She did not have to know what her family, Joseph, or the townspeople would think. She simply replied, "Be it unto me according to thy word."

Has God shown you something and you know it is Him beyond the shadow of a doubt? I'm talking about a word He has given-you couldn't have made it up. Perhaps like me, you didn't even ask for it, but you have Divine confirmation. And even though you have Divine confirmation, things aren't making sense. Things don't look good. You may not understand exactly how God is going to bring this thing He has shown you to pass. I'm encouraging you and myself that our God specializes in things that are impossible!

Impossibility is actually His specialty! We are talking about God, the OMNIPOTENT! The One who calls things that are not as though they were! El Shaddai!! The Almighty God!!! Trust and lean on Him and His word! I know it's hard when you can't see it. But He doesn't want you to see it. That messes it up for Him if you can see how it's going to work out. That's not a big enough thing for Him to step into if you can see it. He wants something only HE can see! And He wants you to trust

Him for it.

Without faith it is impossible to please to Him. That means your circumstance has to be something that doesn't make any sense, but you still step out on the Word anyway. I'm encouraging you and I'm encouraging myself. Let's wake up every day, decreeing and declaring that thing. Let's speak it and seal it with - He said it and that settles it! Be it unto me according to thy Word…be it unto me according to thy Word…be it unto me according to thy Word. Mission Impossible is POSSIBLE when my special secret agent is Jesus!!

Let's pray…

I call on you, Almighty God. I call on you to come in the room where the altar of my heart abides. Lord, I know you are the God of the Impossible. You are the God of miracles, signs, and wonders. You made the ground of the Red Sea dry for the Israelites to cross over. You caused Gideon to win a battle with only 300 men. You caused Jehoshaphat and his armies to triumph, and all they had to do was praise. You quickened Sarah's womb in her old age and made the barren fertile. You raised Lazarus from the dead after 4 days. You move mountains that seem unclimbable. You specialize in things that are impossible. Lord, speak to my heart right now. Speak to my heart what your will is for my life. Speak to my heart what your promise is for my life. And if that thing that you speak seems impossible, despite lack of fraternal support, help me to stand on your word as God of the Impossible. Help me to be confident and assured that what you are doing in me shall manifest. Help me stand courageously despite odds; stand not in the facts, but the truth – that it is already done! And I ask like Job for you to help me wait until my change comes. God of the Impossible, breathe on me. God of the

Impossible, rest on me. God of the Impossible, shine through me. In the name of Jesus, I pray. Amen. So it is.

V

FAITH FIGHT

DEVOTION 14: RESURRECTION TO FERTILITY

Ezekiel 37:1-10 The hand of the LORD was on me, and he brought me out by the Spirit of the LORD and set me in the middle of a valley; it was full of bones. He led me back and forth among them, and I saw a great many bones on the floor of the valley, bones that were very dry. He asked me, "Son of man, can these bones live?" I said, "Sovereign LORD, you alone know." Then he said to me, "Prophesy to these bones and say to them, 'Dry bones, hear the word of the LORD! This is what the Sovereign LORD says to these bones: I will make breath enter you, and you will come to life. I will attach tendons to you and make flesh come upon you and cover you with skin; I will put breath in you, and you will come to life. Then you will know that I am the LORD.'" So I prophesied as I was commanded. And as I was prophesying, there was a noise, a rattling sound, and the bones came together, bone to bone. I looked, and tendons and flesh appeared on them and skin covered them, but there was no breath in them. Then he said to me, "Prophesy to the breath; prophesy, son of man, and say to it, 'This is what the Sovereign LORD says: Come, breath, from the four winds and breathe into these slain, that they may live.'" So I prophesied as he commanded me, and breath entered them; they came to life and stood up on their feet—a vast army. (New International Version)

As I am writing this devotion, I am writing for myself. There is something dead in my life that needs resurrecting. I am walking a faith walk unlike I have ever done before. This devotion I dedicate to my valley experience…

Seeing that this is a woman's devotional, and I am writing about fertility, you would think that the text would be from one of the Bible female greats' stories. But God kept leading me to Ezekiel 37.

In this text is the familiar story of the prophet Ezekiel who wrote of God taking him out by the Spirit and sitting him in a valley full of dry bones. Not only does God place him amongst dead bodies, but there is nothing left of the bodies but bones, and they are very dry. Observe that it is the Lord who set him in the valley. Why would God put one in such a place? Why did He put Ezekiel in in that dry, dead place? Sometimes we put ourselves in bad situations. But there are times that God will set you into low land, into a gulley, into a valley.

When Ezekiel looked at the place, he saw it full of many bones. Merriam-Webster defines word bone(s), being plural, as a dead body and is indicative of a cadaver or corpse. So, here Ezekiel is amongst bodies that have been dead for a very long time. Not only does God place him amongst dead bodies, but there is nothing left of the bodies but bones, and they are very dry.

This is not a 4-day-old corpse like that of Lazarus, but these corpses have been dead for a very long time. Have you ever experienced something that has been seemingly dead for a very long time? Well, I have. And I wonder, why does God have me in this dead situation for so long? What is the purpose? I'm sure Ezekiel was confused about his purpose in being in this place.

The text says that God then asks, "Can these bones live?" What??? Now, Lord, you know what I see is good and dead. You know that I have no power to diagnose the ability for resurrection. I don't have the power to diagnose anything. Ezekiel answers, "Lord, you know." Ezekiel knows not to underestimate the Almighty. He knows that El Shaddai is the only One who could do something about it, so he gave the situation to Him. Perhaps, like I, you have a situation that is too big for you. Do you know what we need to do? Give the situation to Him. Go to the altar, lay it at His feet, and let Him have His way with it.

When the situation is given to God, He can tell you what you need to do about it. He tells Ezekiel to prophesy to the bones and speak them into existence. God could very well have done what He wanted to the bones Himself, but He desires for Ezekiel to do the speaking. Once you turn your will over to God's will, He will instruct you on what to speak. Speaking what you want is not going to work. **You have to make sure you hear what God says and speak what He told you.**

Let me say that again. You have to make sure you hear what God says and speak what He told you.

God will give you the power to call what you do not see into existence-if it is His will. When Ezekiel opens his mouth, the bones are still dead. He has NO inkling of anything having changed with his eyes, but He prophesies anyway.

Let me tell you, there is NO inkling at all that anything in my situation has changed. I mean, there is not a peep of life into it. There is not a peep of any possibility. The only hope I have is in what God told me. I have been struggling with it because what He told me and what I'm experiencing are at odds. But **Romans 4** reminds me that God called things that were not as though they were with Abraham. So, no matter how many ups and downs I have in my self analysis, I will prophesy what God told me anyway.

While Ezekiel was prophesying - I said 'while' –there was a noise and rattling sound. When you begin to prophesy in the power given you, you'll hear a shaking, a rattling, and then you will know–He's putting it all together. When Ezekiel heard the noise, the bones came together bone to bone. Even though they came together, they were still not alive. Coming together was not enough. The connection was not going to make them productive. You can be connected and still be barren, dead, and unfruitful.

So was the case with Hannah, Sarah, and Rachel. Each of these three women in the Bible connected with the seed, but the connection was not enough to make them fertile. In those times, for a woman to not be fertile was such reproach that it often made her feel useless.

In **I Samuel 1**, Hannah is loved more by her husband, Elkanah, than the other wife, Peninnah. Even though it was evident that Elkanah loved Hannah more, not being able to bear children had her in a most distraught mental and spiritual state. Hannah went in prayer so much so at the temple that the priest thought she was drunk because her lips were moving, but no words were coming out. When she spoke, she pleaded her case to God and the priest. The priest prophesied, and Hannah's dead situation began to turn around.

Sarah got into God's business trying to handle things because she was tired of waiting on the promise. She gave Hagar to Abraham to have a child with. Her infertility caused her great distress, but God was going to do what He said He would do. She just had to wait for it.

Rachel knew her husband loved her. He worked 14 years just to get her, but **Genesis 30:1** tells us she said, "Give me children or I will die!" Do you ever feel like that? Like if you remain in your infertile situation, you will die?

I declare that we shall live and not die. According to **Psalm 118:17**, we will declare the works of the Lord. In situations too big for you, I'm talking about problems where you have no power to give life-give it to God. There is no sense in being anxious about it.

My prayer is not to be depressed about it. As a woman, there are times that you experience turmoil inside, longing for birth. That longing can be for the birth of a child or marriage, the rebirth of a relationship, or something else. This is natural for inside us is an instinct for nurturing, carrying, and birthing. Sometimes, we desire to nurture and carry every dry thing in our lives we come across, even things not always in our plight.

However, there are some things that nobody, but you and God, know your womb is groaning for.

I'm talking about a groaning that won't let you sleep at night. A groaning that stretches your spiritual womb. A groaning that gives you nausea because your spirit isn't settled in that infertile situation. A groaning that feels like contractions. When you feel this groaning, sisters, talk to the Man that can bring life to your dead situation. Talk to the Man who can tell you what to speak and when to speak it.

You can't put the bones together. You can't bring flesh onto the bones. And you can't breathe life into them. You can't make them be what you want them to be. You can't even make them be what God wants them to be until He endows you with the power to do it. Talk to the Lord to determine what His desire is. Is the situation dead, or is it capable of becoming viable again? You need to talk to the only Man who has the power to bring resurrection to your infertility.

Let's pray...

Spirit of the Living God, fall fresh upon us right now. Meet us where we are right now, Lord. You are the Omnipotent God, and we praise you! We lift your mighty name! You are the God who can heal and deliver. And as we battle in this faith fight, we ask that you take us out of ourselves, Lord. Put your hand upon us and take us in the Spirit where we can talk with you alone. Show us what you want to show us about our dead situation. Talk to us, Lord, about our dead situation. Open our eyes to our dead situation. And if there is anything for us to speak, Lord, tell us what to speak to our dead situation. We no longer want to walk around expressing our desires for you to grant. We want to say only what you tell us to speak to our situation. Let us echo the words from Your Holy Spirit and send the wind, Lord, to breathe on it. Only your words. At the time you give. With the power only you can provide. Help us in our groaning moments until you take us to that place in you where your will and your power be revealed. Hear our cries, O Lord. For we are crying out to you. It hurts, God. It hurts, and sometimes the tears won't stop. Only you can do something about it, Lord. Meet us. Cradle us. Settle us on who and whose we are. Settle us on the fact that you won't let us dehydrate in our dry, desert situations. In your way... in your time... you will resurrect us to fertility. Lord, we promise to be careful to acknowledge you as the lone operator of our miracle. We exercise this faith in you, your word, and your power. And we seal it in the majestic name of Jesus the Christ, our Lord. Amen.

DEVOTION 15:NO TIME TO MISCARRY

Matthew 11:1-5 And it came to pass, when Jesus had made an end of commanding his twelve disciples, he departed thence to teach and to preach in their cities. Now when John had heard in the prison the works of Christ, he sent two of his disciples, And said unto him, Art thou he that should come, or do we look for another? Jesus answered and said unto them, Go and shew John again those things which ye do hear and see: The blind receive their sight, and the lame walk, the lepers are cleansed, and the deaf hear, the dead are raised up, and the poor have the gospel preached to them. (King James Version)

So many times, in life, God has shown us things. But unfortunately, if it is not packaged how we want, coming to us in the form that we desire, or as soon as we want, we will give up on it. We will miscarry. Physically, a miscarriage occurs when the female's body rejects the fetus prematurely–before it is what we call viable (able to live outside of the womb). The woman's womb is the incubator necessary to hold the baby until the time for delivery.

In life, God will give us revelation of some things. Our job is to be the incubator to nurture and protect the vision until delivery time.

Look at the text. John the Baptist knew all too well who Jesus really was. Remember, John felt the Holy Spirit in his mother's womb! So how could he not know that Jesus was the Messiah? Well, John finds himself in a rough spot. He was in prison, and things weren't looking like he expected. In fact, probably quite the opposite.

He was probably saying, "Now, Jesus, we are cousins. I have baptized you and done all of this and all of that, leading people to you. Do you mean to tell me that you can't do anything about me being in this prison?" He was so ticked about it that he sent word to Jesus. He told messengers, "Go straight to him and point-blank ask him. Are you the one, or is it somebody else I need to be looking for because you sholl ain't acting like you are the one?"

Jesus gave him a simple answer. "John, The blind see; the lame walk. Lepers are clean now. The deaf hear. I'm raising people from the dead, and the poor have the gospel preached to them." Jesus did not feel the need to give John any more insight into the details of the journey because He knew He had already done enough.

If you are in a situation like John right now and you doubt the vision God gave you, don't miscarry. Please make sure the vision was from God and not a fairy tale you put together. If it was indeed from Him, don't miscarry now. The baby (vision) needs you.

I heard a preacher say one time that a woman is a receptacle in a relationship with her husband. Like a cord must have a plug (receptacle) to give birth to power, a woman is a receptacle, giving birth to the bloom the man will become. This is true on so many more levels than marriage, though.

YOU are the receptacle the vision is to bud from. Hold on to it until God says it is time. Don't put yourself in danger of miscarrying like John and miss the blessing.

I'm reminded of Hans Christian Anderson's "The Nightingale." An emperor heard about a nightingale in his kingdom, famous for its voice. He asked for the nightingale to come to the palace for him. He was surprised that it was a drab-looking gray bird, but it sang the most beautiful song. One day, a gift arrived that was an imitation of the nightingale, made of gold and full of jewels. The nightingale did not seem as unique a gift as before. The nightingale left, and the emperor was left with the imitation.

Sometimes we can get so caught up in what others have that seems better than what we have or looks better to the eye that we let the real thing go. The original may be drab, but don't let it go if it is what God gave you in the vision. When the imitation fell apart, the emperor was sick unto death. Sometimes letting the vision go will make you spiritually, deathly sick. You may go through symptoms of miscarrying in the spirit.

Later in the story, the emperor became sick and needed the healing power of the original nightingale's song. Luckily, a young girl in the castle got the nightingale to come back and sing for the emperor. When he did, the emperor was made new.

Let me be the girl in the story for you. Pray and allow the Holy Spirit to bring the remembrance of the vision God gave for you to carry. You may be in a rough spot right now, and it doesn't seem like your vision is authentic. Or maybe it doesn't look like it's much worth it.

But remember the servants at the wedding in Cana. They drew water from the well when they were out of wine. It was water in the well and water when they poured it into the pot. We don't know which step along the way it turned into wine. But Jesus spoke over it! Somewhere along the walk, before pouring the water out, it was made wine. And not just any kind of wine, but it was the best wine they'd ever tasted. You are on your walk along the way. If you give up now, prematurely, the baby (vision) will not be able to live on its own yet and will surely die. Hold on to the vision. Nurture it. Speak life into it. Call those things that are not as though they were. Watch God work it out! This is no time to miscarry!

Let's pray…

We thank you, Lord God, for your vision. Habukkuk 2 tells us that though the vision tarry, we are to wait for it. It will show up at its appointed time. Let us not grow weary as we fight this fight of faith, Lord. Let us not get frustrated, angry, or doubtful of the vision you gave us. Help us to allow the vision its incubation period and hold on to you and it during this time. Grow us, Lord, to have that staying power. We know Satan will distract us with things around us that look better than what you gave us and what you told us to wait for, but we cancel distractions in the name of Jesus. We bring every thought into captivity that does not measure up to the knowledge of Christ. When we lose focus, steer us back on the right path. Don't let us miscarry the vision prematurely. We do not want to be like the children of Israel at the edge of the Promised Land and never able to partake of it because of listening to false reports. Help us to walk it out until our water turns into wine. Help us carry the vision to full term and through the birthing process, where we shall enjoy the pleasantries of your goodness in the land of the living. We love you, and we praise you in advance. In Jesus' name, we pray. So shall it be.

DEVOTION 16: CLAIMING YOUR INTERSECTION

Genesis 33:22-42 That night Jacob got up and took his two wives, his two female servants, and his eleven sons and crossed the ford of the Jabbok. After he had sent them across the stream, he sent over all his possessions. So Jacob was left alone, and a man wrestled with him till daybreak. When the man saw that he could not overpower him, he touched the socket of Jacob's hip so that his hip was wrenched as he wrestled with the man. Then the man said, "Let me go, for it is daybreak." But Jacob replied, "I will not let you go unless you bless me." The man asked him, "What is your name?" "Jacob," he answered. Then the man said, "Your name will no longer be Jacob, but Israel, because you have struggled with God and with humans and have overcome." Jacob said, "Please tell me your name." But he replied, "Why do you ask my name?" Then he blessed him there. So Jacob called the place Peniel, saying, "It is because I saw God face to face, and yet my life was spared." The sun rose above him as he passed Peniel, and he was limping because of his hip. Therefore to this day the Israelites do not eat the tendon attached to the socket of the hip, because the socket of Jacob's hip was touched near the tendon. (New International Version)

I was on my way home from work and needed to make a few

stops, even though there was pending bad weather. When I was through with my errands and got back on the road, I was in a hurry. I was in a 'Left Only' turning lane, and cars were coming, so I couldn't turn. I was in such haste to get where I was going that I said to myself, "I am going to claim my intersection."

I moved forward so that no one could go on the green light even when the light turned red on me until I made my turn first. I was not going to let my opportunity to move on toward my destination be prolonged. In my spirit, I thought of Jacob.

Jacob was troubled on his way to meet his brother Esau for the first time in many years. He knew that meeting his brother after tricking him might not be pleasant. When Jacob left home years before, Esau sought to kill him. But he needed to connect back with his brother, and he needed for things to be well.

Have you ever been troubled about something? It may not be that you have done anything wrong, but you know you are destined to be connected to someone or something more. Yet, there is something negative blocking your way. Whatever it is, perhaps you can liken it to cars that keep going on a road preventing you from turning left, which is where you need to go to reach your destination.

When the roadblocks are set, and fear has you bound, what would you do? Some just stay in their position on the road. Perhaps, they may even turn around and choose to go back to where they came from or look for an easier destination to get to. I have done both. Stayed stagnant in fear and let fear allow me to put my car in reverse.

But this year, I have gotten to a point where I just KNOW that I cannot postpone my journey to my destiny any longer. And the only way I can get there is to turn left in this lane. To be honest, it would be so much easier to just abort this assignment. But I can't. HE (God) won't let me. There is a burning, yearning, feverish, vehement boiling of passion for this purpose inside of me that I cannot control. I wish I could put it out, but I can't. So, I will have to fight the entire course to get to my destination. I don't feel like it, but there literally is no other option.

This is how Jacob must've felt. He had been through so much hell that there was no turning back. His fear caused him to send gifts to appease Esau. He even strategically split his family so that one group might be able to escape, if necessary. After putting all these strategies in place, he knew, though, he could not succeed without the help of God. So he spent the night by himself, wrestling with a man, and took the opportunity to *claim his intersection*. He spent the entire night wrestling with a man.

Have you ever spent a sleepless night wrestling with God about something? If you did, did you know how to properly claim the intersection? I can't tell you exactly what techniques to use. All I can tell you is that what stood out to me in the text is the **24th verse**. Specifically, it was the part where it says he wrestled 'until the breaking of the day.'

It doesn't matter how long the night is. You can't quit tussling in the spirit. Sometimes, you get to a point where you just can't stand to stay in the same position you've been in. You are tired of being tired of where you are. When you know it's past time to make a move, you must *claim your intersection*.

Jacob was such a formidable opponent in the match that the man moved Jacob's thigh out of joint to end it. Yes, there was breaking during the wrestling.

When you wrestle with God, you see how low you are and how magnanimous He is! Of course, your spirit will be broken, and your heart humbled before Him, but that is precisely the sacrifice it takes to please Him (**Psalm 51**)! When you bare yourself before Him, that is the first step in positioning your vehicle in the intersection.

The text reveals that you must wait for God to initiate a conversation with you. The man told Jacob to let him go, for it was daybreak. But Jacob refused to let go until the man/angel blessed him. You must **refuse** to take no for an answer sometimes. When you are in the spirit and have reached that pinnacle, you will know what to say to get God to move on your behalf.

In this text, God changed Jacob's name. He would no longer be Jacob (trickster), but His name would be Israel (Prince). God can and will turn things around.

First: you must psych yourself up for the fight. Once you have made the decision in your mind to fight, consider this. Do you think wrestlers or boxers work out once a week, and that's all the preparation they need for the big fight? Oh no! It takes discipline for weeks and months to prepare them for the one big fight. Prayer and the Word are the exercises you need for the fight. When you talk with the Lord, you need to be able to speak His language. You can't do that when you haven't spent time with Him or in His Word.

I had to literally create a War Room for this fight I'm in, just like the movie. The Word is on the wall in my room. The Word is on the wall in my office at work. Prayer and worship in the morning on the way to work. Prayer when I get to work. Prayer on my break. The Word instead of the radio in my car. Prayer and worship when I go walking. Prayer and worship in the middle of the night when I wake up.

When you have a stirring in your spirit and want God to move, you will consume yourself with Him. And even when it doesn't seem to be working, something won't let you quit until He comes through.

Do you remember the 10th chapter of Daniel? Daniel had been in mourning and fasting for 3 whole weeks when an angel came to him in a vision. The angel told him, "From the first day you set your heart and humbled yourself before God, your words were heard, and I was on my way to you! But the Prince of the kingdom of Persia (an evil spirit) was fighting me and withheld me from coming to you. The angel Michael had to come to help me! But you kept praying, and now there is a Word for you."

Do you get it? You must wrestle because you don't know what your angels are fighting in the spiritual realm to deliver your breakthrough! You've come too far to turn around!! You must take the first step of faith and claim your intersection. Wrestle as long as you have to and watch God work it out!

Let's pray…

O Lord God, I desire your presence. I want communion with you, Lord. There are some things that I cannot ask an intercessor to go to you for on my behalf. It's between you and me. You know my uprisings and my down fallings. You know me better than I know myself. You know what my spirit is troubled about. You know what I have come to you about. You know the end you have prepared for me concerning this thing. Lord, I need to hear from you, and I won't let you go about this thing until you bless me concerning it. I come to you because you have the power to grant me success in this situation. You have the power to reroute things. You can modify what Satan has set. I am yours, Lord, and you know my destiny concerning this situation. I am praying that you make it right, and I will keep coming to you until you do. I am praying that you elevate me, change my name if you must, and I'm going to keep coming to you until you do. My destiny seems to be held up, but I am claiming the intersection. I want what is mine. Deliver me from this dormant state. I've come too far, Lord, to turn around. I can't give up now. So, until you turn this situation, it's you and me. It's you and me. Commune with me, God. Show me more of you. Show me your plans for me and what you will have me do. Your word says that I am to wait until my change comes. So right here, at this intersection, that is what I am going to do. Don't leave me, Lord. You may have to break me. But I know you are The Potter, and you can put me back together again—a brand-new vessel. I declare your unmatched power and presence at this intersection in my life, and I thank you in advance. In the name of Jesus, I pray. Amen

DEVOTION 17: WHEN ALL IS QUIET ON THE SET

Psalm 22: 1-11, 14-15, 19-22 For the director of music. To the tune of "The Doe of the Morning." A psalm of David. My God, my God, why have you forsaken me? Why are you so far from saving me, so far from my cries of anguish? My God, I cry out by day, but you do not answer, by night, but I find no rest. Yet you are enthroned as the Holy One; you are the one Israel praises. In you our ancestors put their trust; they trusted and you delivered them. To you they cried out and were saved; in you they trusted and were not put to shame. But I am a worm and not a man, scorned by everyone, despised by the people. All who see me mock me; they hurl insults, shaking their heads. "He trusts in the LORD," they say, "let the LORD rescue him. Let him deliver him, since he delights in him." Yet you brought me out of the womb; you made me trust in you, even at my mother's breast. From birth I was cast on you; from my mother's womb you have been my God. Do not be far from me, for trouble is near and there is no one to help...I am poured out like water, and all my bones are out of joint. My heart has turned to wax; it has melted within me. My mouth is dried up like a potsherd, and my tongue sticks to the roof of my mouth; you lay me in the dust of death...But you, LORD, do not be far

from me. You are my strength; come quickly to help me. Deliver me from the sword, my precious life from the power of the dogs. Rescue me from the mouth of the lions; save me from the horns of the wild oxen. I will declare your name to my people; in the assembly I will praise you. (New International Version)

Have you ever felt like you were in a place alone? And not only was there no one in the earthly realm by your side but that even God had left you, too? It may be considered impolite to say that, for we know the Word says He will never leave us nor forsake us.

But the transparent truth is that I have felt this way. And I'm probably sure you have, too. I have felt like I was in a pit, like a sewer with no light, and only the echo of my moans and cries. I did not feel like God was there. I had prayed and cried, and prayed and cried, and prayed and cried. And I heard…absolutely nothing. Didn't hear anything. Didn't feel anything. Didn't see anything. In a recent moment like this, I asked myself: Where is God? Where is He? It feels like all is quiet on the set.

All is quiet on the set. Quiet on the set. That's not a term I hear very often. I don't even know where in the file cabinet of my memory it came from at that moment. But there it was.

All is quiet on the set. In filmmaking, the Director may announce, "Quiet on the set!" when the next scene begins. During a 'quiet on the set,' all voices are hushed. Not even whispers or cell phones vibrating are allowed to disturb the scene. You don't want to hear the whispers or the vibrating phones in the background while recording. You don't want the whispers or the vibrating to distract the actors and actresses as they play their roles. The only thing for everyone to do is perform their role in time during the scene until the scene is cut. Let me say that again. **The only thing for everyone to do is perform their role in time during the scene until the scene is cut**. Here is what was revealed to me about this.

When all is quiet, and you are begging for God to give you an answer, and you hear nothing from His voice-first, give homage to Him as the Director of the film. The Director doesn't even talk while all is quiet on the set and recording is taking place. The Director has already given instructions to all cast members on where to stand, how to project, place lighting here, zoom in there, etc. God has given you some instructions already. Have you heeded those instructions? Do you even remember what He said? If you don't, ask the Holy Spirit to bring back to your remembrance what He gave you. If you haven't heeded the instructions, you know you have work to do.

Your job is to be obedient and trust that the Director knows what He is doing. He knows just how the movie is going to end. The Director knows if He needs to speak to you because you aren't producing what He's looking for. So, if He's not saying anything to you, keep doing what you have been doing.

If that is praying and crying and being broken before Him, keep doing it. If that is standing still, waiting to see His salvation in a situation, be steadfast and unmovable despite the silence! Sometimes, you just must let the scene play out. You may not be the star of this scene. Just play your part and trust in Him who holds the worlds and you in His hands.

This passage of Psalm was believed to have been written by David. It is sometimes recited during the Feast of Esther in the Jewish faith tradition. What sticks out most is the first verse with the infamous words, "My God, my God! Why have you forsaken me?"

Some feel this was prophetic of what Jesus would say on the cross. Some feel Jesus was reciting the Davidic text from memory because of what He was enduring on the cross. The question is asked by philosophers at this point on the cross: "Well, if Jesus is God and He and His Father are one, how could Jesus be separated from God?"

We may not be able to comprehend the details, but we know that Jesus felt separation from His Father on the cross. He even asked the question Himself. "Where are you, Father? Why have you left me alone? I've never been without you. How could you turn your back on me?"

All this was necessary for Jesus to pull from within Himself and produce in His purpose as the Messiah. Likewise, God is inside of you, breathed into you. You need to reach down in your spirit to that part of Him deep within and pull it out! Or, as Paul told Timothy, stir up the gift within you. In the stirring of that within, you will produce what the Director wants to see come out of you.

The person in the text has found himself in a severe form of anguish and pain. He speaks of crying, day and night, and hearing nothing. Been there, done that! He acknowledges God as the God of his forefathers and acknowledges God's exceptional winning record in history with them, and states they were not put to shame. This person obviously feels like he is being put to shame, though. Been there, done that!

He says, "Lord, I am only a worm! People talk about me and despise me, insult me, and mock me because I'm yours! They even say that since I profess to be your child, how come you have allowed this treacherous thing to happen to me?"

I have certainly felt like this person. I told on my enemies-"Lord, they mock me and say she's God's, so let God help her!" I have wept-"I'm branded by you, God, and you must come to help me! Don't let me be made ashamed, Lord!"

The truth is that in these situations, we are not always at our strongest. Sometimes, we allow the negativity of our adversaries to be the whispers and vibrating that distract us from our role in the scene.

Whew! Somebody needed to hear that! Don't you dare allow the whispers and vibrating to disturb the scene of your Director! Cast down every argument and high thing that exalts itself against the knowledge of God and bring every thought into captivity to the obedience of Christ! Send it back to Hell from where it came and tell Satan, "You have no place here!" Now back to the text...

After issuing the complaint, the person in the text says, "Lord, you have been my God from the beginning. I don't even know another God. From my mother's womb you were my God! I ain't fixing to put you down and search for another. You are who I know, and it is to You that I come! Rescue me! Don't be far from me, God! Move quickly! You are my strength! Come on, Jesus, and see about me!"

The text teaches that even when He is quiet on the set, continue to put your faith and trust in Him. Let Him know that you are expecting Him to come. It's hard to do at times, but I know there is no other name on earth I can call on. Nor do I even want to try another.

I have to tell Him, "Even when I can't see, can't hear, can't feel, God, I know you hear me. And I can't take any more." I'm surprised I find comfort in David not telling us how God comes to deliver. In the last ten verses, though, we find out that He does come through!! Hallelujah! Perhaps, David doesn't even see the deliverance yet, but goes ahead and praises because He knows that God WILL deliver-no ifs, ands, or buts about it.

I say that because David moves from saying "rescue me" in one sentence to "I will declare your name in the assembly and praise you!" If you pour your heart out to God long enough, declare who He is and what He's capable of doing, and then move to express that you know He's going to do it for you-you will be able to take your place on the set. Keep pressing. Keep believing. Keep doing what God told you to do and watch how God orchestrates the scene to play out! Hallelujah!

Let's pray...
Right now, O Father God, I pray to you in this area where I feel I'm

not hearing from you. I know you desire a broken heart and a contrite spirit. I lay all my ugliness before you. God, I know some mock me. I have declared trust and belief that you will do what you said you would do. It just hasn't manifested from the spiritual realm to the natural realm yet. I feel scorned. I feel ashamed. I feel a fool at times. I don't know how much more broken I can get before I am nothing. I lay this all at your feet. At the feet of my Rock of Ages! At the feet of my Help from ages past and times to come! Like the widow seeking relief from her adversary, I seek for you to vindicate me, God! I am branded with your name, and you must come to my aid! Please, God, help me in this dark time. I know You are mine, and I am yours! Help me stir up the gift within me and pull from that God-part of me so that I can play the role I am to play in this season as you orchestrate this scene. I don't know how, I don't know when, but I know there is No IF! WHEN you deliver me, my adversaries will see who YOU are! Even though it's a press, I praise you now for what I know in my spirit you have spoken that you SHALL do. In the name of Jesus, I lay it all at your feet as I meditate in the 'quiet.'. Amen.

DEVOTION 18:MARINES FIGHT TO WIN

Ephesians 6: 10-13 Finally, be strong in the Lord and in his mighty power. Put on the full armor of God, so that you can take your stand against the devil's schemes. For our struggle is not against flesh and blood, but against the rulers, against the authorities, against the powers of this dark world and against the spiritual forces of evil in the heavenly realms. Therefore, put on the full armor of God, so that when the day of evil comes, you may be able to stand your ground, and after you have done everything, to stand. (New International Version)

On this Christian journey, you will endure different races to run. Various battles to fight in Kingdom War. Everyone has their own battles. The one you may cross in your 20's, someone else may not come upon until their 40's. You must deal with some conflicts that your friends and family may never come upon. But one thing for sure is this-we all have battles.

Merriam-Webster defines battle as a general encounter between armies. It may be an extended struggle to succeed or survive. In this life, you must recognize that there are constantly spiritual battles for you to fight. Battles that the enemy started plotting against you a long time ago. Satan, your arch enemy, knows God's plans and future for you. He has been scheming all your life to keep you from reaching your destiny, your divine promises given to you by God.

In his letter to the Ephesians, Paul writes that you must put on the whole armor of God to take your stand against the tactics of Satan. **Yes, I said take–your–stand**. Of course, you may say, "Well, if God has it for me, I should get it anyway. I shouldn't have to fight for it." But the Word lets us know that way of thinking is contrary.

If Satan has been going to and fro, seeking who he may devour since he got kicked out of Heaven, trust me, you're on his devouring list. If you are one of God's chosen, you are an enemy of Satan. He will try his best to divert you from the blessings of the Lord. Satan tried to divert Jesus from becoming the Christ to save our sins, but it didn't work! Jesus took His stand, and He fought, and He won!

You better believe that Satan is trying to belittle and diminish all who are Christ's until that great battle of Armageddon. Knowing that Satan has declared war on your life, I mean your whole life, I compel you to take your stand spiritually. Take it in the way that the United States Marines speak of taking their stand physically. The perspective that the Marines take is this. Marines fight to win.

In this 6th chapter of Ephesians, Paul equates the spiritual struggle to that of a battle and tells us to get ready to be strong. This indicates that our character must be prepared to weather *extreme, intense pressure* that may cause us to falter or lose hope. A lot of the enemy's tactics to weaken us involve our minds. Philippians 2:5 says that the mind that we hold is to be likened to the mind of Christ Jesus. Christ came on earth for a set purpose, and nothing was going to stop Him, in His humanity, from achieving what He set out to do.

I would suggest that once you have your mind made up for the set purpose God has called you to, you have won half your battle. You must let NOTHING deter you from believing that with God, you can win. Oh, I'm sorry. I mean, you WILL win. You must expect doubt and disappointments, which is part of the battle. Is it not the pitcher's purpose to try to throw a curveball that the batter will miss? Is it not the enemy's purpose to reduce their opponent's confidence? Well, whenever thoughts come to your mind that say you are not good enough, expect it. You must have a counter-thought to speak to your mind. Say instead, "I must be better than good enough for you to try to place this thought in my mind in the first place. Thank you, enemy, for the confirmation that I am good enough. Be gone!" Make up an "antonym phrase" for every evil scheme Satan sends your way.

Proverbs 18:21 says, "Life and death are in the power of the tongue." Open your mouth and speak the Word until it saturates your mind, as you will need when you take your stand. Note that everything I have said in this paragraph is required to battle. The Word. What you think. And what you speak. I will not go into the whole armor of God piece by piece, which is in the rest of Ephesians 6. I want to focus on the base ingredients of-the Word-What you think-And what you speak.

The Word is what Jesus used in his wilderness fight against Satan. Every time Satan tempted his mind and senses with something, Jesus used the Word. If you are currently in a battle and don't know the Word, it is time to dig into it. Pray and search for the scriptures that are relative to your struggle. Write them down or type and print them and post them where you can see them. Yes, make your "War Room."

I am a witness that looking at Scriptures every day and verbalizing them (which is the next step) helped me retain them in my mind. What can beat the Word of God? What can conquer the Word of God? What can prevail against the Word of God? What can overcome the Word of God? Did not God even say Himself that His own Word shall not return unto Him void (**Isaiah 55:11**)? Did He not say that Heaven and Earth shall pass away before His words will (**Matthew 24:45**)? Did God not tell Abram when He made a promise about his seed that He looked around and could not find anything else greater to swear by? So, He swore by His own self that He would do what He said He was going to do (**Genesis 22, Hebrews 6**)! Hallelujah!! That one just blessed me right there.

Do you remember the movie, Superman? Superman knew kryptonite had to be avoided so that his power would not be weakened. Just knowing that there is no kryptonite or element strong enough to dilute the power of His Word is enough to make me shout! Glory be to God!! That makes me want to know more about it. Get in it. Understand it. Seek revelation from it even more. Remember, the first weapon for the fight is His Word.

"For as (a man) thinketh in his heart, so is He..." (**Proverbs 23:7**). What is in your mind saturates your heart. Therefore, it is pertinent that your mind thinks like a conqueror for the win. Wait a minute.

Romans 8:37 says, "Nay, in all these things we are more than conquerors through him that loved us." More than!! Conquerors win, so I must supernaturally win! So, your mind must remain steadfast in that frameset.

Remember **Philippians 4:8**, "Finally, brethren, whatsoever things are true, whatsoever things are honest, whatsoever things are just, whatsoever things are pure, whatsoever things are lovely, whatsoever things are of good report; if there be any virtue, and if there be any praise, think on these things."

If a thought comes into your mind that is not true to what God says, shake your head no and cast it out. If an idea comes that is not honest, or just, or pure, or lovely, or of good report, shake your head no and cast it out. Your mind is too valuable to give time to things not of Godly virtue. The more you dismiss negative thinking, the more your mind is molded into the state it needs to be for the fight.

As I write this devotion, I am in the middle of my own battle. Satan is attacking my mind as I intercede on behalf of my father, who is right now in the hospital, fighting with Covid-19. Here I am, writing to you on how to fight to win, and I, honestly, am experiencing so many daggers thrown at my mind in this fight that I feel unfit to continue to write this devotion. I have almost fainted. Almost. Just almost. BUT, I have had to lean on my own writing and walk it out for myself. I have had to come up with counterattacks for what Satan has put in my mind, particularly this week, unlike any other time in my life.

I've had to say, "God must be coming through for me since you harass my thoughts as much as you do." I will not bow. I will not bend. I will fight to win. So, know that as I write this devotion, it is out of the purity of experience. Yes, I admit I almost fainted. But did not David say the same thing in Psalm 27? I believe he said, "I would have fainted unless I had believed that I would see the goodness of the Lord in the land of the living. Wait on the Lord; be of good courage, and He shall strengthen thine heart. Wait, I say, on the Lord!"

So, please, counterattack whatever negative thinking Satan approaches your mind with. Another slogan in contemporary ads from the Marines cites that battles are won within. Saturate your mind and heart with spiritual warrior thoughts. Thoughts become theory. Then your theory becomes your truth. Your truth must be able to combat the spiritual forces of evil to sustain your position on the battlefront to win.

What you speak. Reference has already been made to Proverbs speaking of death and life in the power of the tongue. What you let come out of your mouth has more power than you know. For what you speak, your ears hear. And what you hear infiltrates your heart and mind within. See, this battle is cyclical in nature.

The Word > I see it. The Word > I think it. The Word > I speak it. I think it > it saturates my inner being. I speak it > I think it > it saturates my inner being. So how I think in my heart > so am I or so it is. Speaking is indeed powerful!

Job 22:28 tells us that you shall decree a thing, and it shall be established unto you. You must decree it! A decree is a statement of what to do that must be obeyed by those concerned (Merriam-Webster). Speak your statement! Open your mouth and vocalize it in the atmosphere! Do you know why this is important? Because your spiritual enemy needs to hear it. Remember, your struggle is not against flesh and blood but against spiritual forces in the dark and evil in heavenly realms.

There are forces in the atmosphere that you cannot physically see, but when the power of your word speaks into the atmosphere, it can repel those forces.

Remember, **II Corinthians 10**–we do not war according to the flesh. The weapons of our warfare are not carnal, but mighty in God for pulling down strongholds, casting down arguments or imaginations, and every high thing that exalts itself against the knowledge of God. Our weapons bring every thought into captivity to the obedience of Christ. To make these forces succumb to you, command their obedience to the Word of God.

It does not matter what it looks like, what is presented to you, what symptoms are present at this time. Speak that you win. You didn't start this battle to give up now! You have come too far to quit! Do you mean to tell me all your struggling this far was for naught? I don't think so! You will not stop until you win! You will not resign until you win! How dare you think it possible to abandon or vacate your position on this battlefield! You will not melt or faint in the presence of the enemy!! You will hold on!! You will persevere!! You will submit to the Word.

Submit what you think and what you speak to the will of God. And with God and God alone–you are in this fight to Win!!!

Let's pray…

O, Father God, I come in the mighty name of your Son Jesus, first of all, saying, Thank you! I love you, Lord! You are worthy of all praise, glory, and honor!!! I pray for every sister who may read this devotion and needs intercession for the battle. I call you El Shaddai-the Almighty God! Be El Shaddai in my sisters' situations right now, Jesus. Let them know that they are not in the battle alone. When their spirit begins to melt, give them the gust of energy to take their stand. Cover their minds and what they think. Cover their eyes and what they see, their ears and what they hear. Let Your Word be supreme in their inner being, God. Remind them of the power in Your blood and Your name. May they call on You during every moment in the battle for reinforcement. Let no weapon that Satan forms against them prosper. No tactic of the enemy shall take root in their lives. Let them know that whatever comes against them, you give them the power to condemn it. Build them up in this very moment to be warrior women, God. Spiritual warriors in the Kingdom. Make them know beyond the shadow of a doubt that it ain't over until You say it's over! Hold on, my sweet sisters! Change is coming! My sisters will see goodness in the land of the living! Things will turn around in the name of Jesus! We decree it. In the name of Jesus, it is so, and so it is! My sisters shall fight until they win!!! Hallelujah!!! We praise your name, Jesus!! In Your name Jesus, we seal this prayer. Amen!!!

DEVOTION 19: THE GIANT IN THE LITTLE MAID

2 Kings 5: 1-4, 14-15 Now Naaman, captain of the host of the king of Syria, was a great man with his master, and honourable, because by him the LORD had given deliverance unto Syria: he was also a mighty man in valour, but he was a leper. And the Syrians had gone out by companies, and had brought away captive out of the land of Israel a little maid; and she waited on Naaman's wife. And she said unto her mistress, Would God my lord were with the prophet that is in Samaria! for he would recover him of his leprosy. And one went in, and told his lord, saying, Thus and thus said the maid that is of the land of Israel...Then went he down, and dipped himself seven times in Jordan, according to the saying of the man of God: and his flesh came again like unto the flesh of a little child, and he was clean. And he returned to the man of God, he and all his company, and came, and stood before him: and he said, Behold, now I know that there is no God in all the earth, but in Israel: (King James Version)

An old idiom states, "Don't judge a book by its cover." It implies that sometimes what you see on the outside does not reveal the worth of what it is inside. Such is the case in the text of this devotion. This can be seen in a popular Old Testament story, the story of Naaman.

Naaman, the main character, is the captain of the Syrian army, which was formidable in its day. His high rank and position with his master placed him in a position of authority and clout. Despite the accolades given to Naaman, he has an issue. Leprosy has struck his body. Leprosy was a term for contagious, deplorable skin diseases in the Bible that caused its hosts to be shunned by society. With all the power and influence he had; he could not fix this issue in his life. Naaman's army was notorious for its feats and had brought captives from God's chosen house of Israel. Naaman got one of the captives, referred to as "a little maid" in the King's James Version, and the young girl served Naaman's wife.

Who is this little maid? What tribe of Israel did she come from? Exactly how old was she? What was her name? Theologians often refer to her as "the girl with no name." One would think–is she even worth mentioning if it was not important enough to know her name?

Let me stop right here and say something. It does not matter who does not know your name. The very essence of who you are is enough to make a mark, like our friend here. When looking at this 5th chapter, there are 27 verses. She is only mentioned in 3 of these verses. That's only 1/9 or 11% of the chapter. Yet, her role is gigantic in the plot. She is a captive. A servant. A slave. She owns nothing. In fact, someone owns her. She is to do as she is told. She is away from her homeland. Away from her family. Forced to attend to Naaman's wife at her every beck and call. But even in her anonymity and situation, she chimes on about her God and his prophet. Even in her anonymity and position, she is considerate and cares for those who hold her bound. She cries to Naaman's wife, "I wish to God that Lord Naaman was with the prophet in Samaria! He would be fully recovered of his leprosy!" She speaks…

There is power when she speaks. There is power in what she says. She is little. She is only a maid. But what she speaks has power. Naaman got wind of what this anonymous little maid declared. It caused him to seek permission from his master to search for the prophet in Israel. I will not go into how indignant Naaman was when he got to the prophet, for Naaman is not the main character to me.

What matters to me is that he went off the word of the little maid to get the word of the prophet. And when he moved on the prophet's word, his healing came! Yes sir!! Did you hear what I just said? If it were not for the word of the little maid, his healing never would have come!! Not only his healing, but spiritual deliverance came for him, too!! Read the whole chapter some time and note the printed verse above that where he stated, "Behold, I know that there is no God in all the earth, but in Israel!!" Hallelujah!!

There may be some woman out there right now that feels little. You may be young, like the girl in the text. You may be middle-aged or a seasoned woman. You do not have to be the age of a young girl to feel small. You do not have to be in the young girl's occupation to feel like you are in a lesser position than someone else. These feelings are quite natural and come to us women from time to time in various situations. You may feel little on your job, in your home, in your family, in ministry, or in a relationship. Satan uses his weapon of comparison with us to create doubt about our value and worth.

But I serve Satan notice. I command him to go back to Hell, for he has no authority in my territory! He has ABSOLUTELY NO POWER to declare 'little' or 'less than' over you or me!! In fact, he discerns what is concealed inside of us. He attacks our thoughts and feelings in hopes that we do not recognize the beauty of what is within.

In his second letter to Corinth, Paul penned that we have a treasure in these earthly vases! We have the light, the knowledge of God's glory through Christ Jesus, and when we have that on the inside…baby, let me tell you…we have ENOUGH!!! If God is for us, tell me who can be against us (**Romans 8:31**)?

You may be in a predicament right now, making you feel like a little maid, but because you are His, there is a giant within!! Yes, I said GIANT!!! In **Psalm 139** this morning, I read where the Word told me I was fearfully and wonderfully made! I know His works are marvelous, and since He created me, that makes me exquisite!! You are splendid, too! I encourage you, sister, to be like the little maid.

You do not need a man's title or position. You do not need a man's recognition or affirmation. Speak for yourself about who God is and what He can do!! Speak what was told to the little maid Mary in **Luke 1** that nothing shall be impossible with God!!

Speak what Job said in **Job 42**: "I know that you can do all things; no purpose of yours can be thwarted."

Speak from **Galatians 4** that you are a daughter of the Kings of Kings, making you a royal heir! Yes, you may have an issue like Naaman. You may have two or three issues. It Does Not Matter! I know someone else who had an issue.

Speak like another anonymous sister from **Matthew 9** that had an issue of blood! The Bible says she kept saying within herself, "If I could just touch the hem of His garment, I will be made whole!" You have a weapon inside of you, Sis!! Quit concealing it!! Let the giant woman of God in you speak!! The giant in you has influence! The giant in you has **spiritual potency**! The giant in you is **packed with power**!! But what good is a weapon if you don't use it?

I am reminded of a cartoon I watched when I was young about a young lady named Princess Adora. She did not know her identity. She was kidnapped, helpless, held captive, and mindcontrolled by an evil captain. But one day, it was revealed to her who she really was. She started believing she was more than initially thought. She was more than what others told her and more than what her situation looked like. When her self-identity changed, the spell of mind-control over her was broken! Whenever a problem presented itself, she would reach into the back of her outfit and pull out her sword and speak, "I have the power!" She was transformed into the heroine we know as She-Ra.

Pull out your sword, Sis! There's a **heroine** in you, girl! There's

power from on high in you, girl! There is a **transformation** waiting to happen in you, girl! There's healing and deliverance for someone in your path within you, girl! There's healing and deliverance for you if you just reach within yourself and stir up the gift, girl! Believe it!! Speak it!!! Let loose the giant in the little maid!!!!

Let's pray…

Father God, we come boldly before your throne as your daughters. We are heirs to the promises of Abraham and joint-heirs with Christ. We dare not waste your sacrifice on the cross, allowing us access to the throne room to get what we need. Facts may be that we appear little or less than due to our current situations, but what we know is who and whose we are! There is fire on the inside of this girl. There is a treasure on the inside of this girl. There is anointing on the inside of this girl. We pull out our swords to fight with that. That is your word. Deuteronomy 28 says that if we hearken diligently unto your voice, observe and do all your commandments, you will set us on high above all nations of the earth. We are not perfect, but we have heard your voice and obeyed your commandments. We declare our blessings and promises to sprout forth. We speak that nothing you have for us is allowable for the enemy to keep. We declare that when we speak your promises, they are yea and amen. We decree that we have more than the world against us with you for us. Spirit of the Living God, where we see little, show us the giant. Where we see little, reveal the supernatural Holy Ghost power within. Where we see little, give us confidence and assurance that we have influence in us. Help us be resolute in our stand that Satan has no power where You have dominion. We do not step out on our own but in your presence, protection, and power. We fight with faith as giants. We go ahead and give you worthy praise for victory. It is so.

In the name of Jesus, we pray and ask all things. Amen.

VI

FOR THE MAIDENS

DEVOTION 20: HE MAY GO AROUND THE WORLD, BUT HE'LL FIND YOU

Genesis 24:12-15a And he said, O LORD God of my master Abraham, I pray thee, send me good speed this day, and shew kindness unto my master Abraham. Behold, I stand here by the well of water; and the daughters of the men of the city come out to draw water: And let it come to pass, that the damsel to whom I shall say, Let down thy pitcher, I pray thee, that I may drink; and she shall say, Drink, and I will give thy camels drink also: let the same be she that thou hast appointed for thy servant Isaac; and thereby shall I know that thou hast shewed kindness unto my master. And it came to pass, before he had done speaking, that, behold, Rebekah came out... (King James Version)

This devotion is for all my single sisters in Christ. I'm referencing here, as earlier, "The Princess and the Pea" parable. Remember that the story starts off with a prince who traveled worldwide for his princess and couldn't find one. He found plenty of princesses, but there was always something not quite right about them, something wrong. He could never determine if they were real or not. Note the princess in the story. She doesn't even know that the prince is looking for a wife when she shows up the night of the storm.

If she knew that, she might've sought shelter somewhere else and got a change of clothes first. Destiny would have it that she knocked on this particular town's gate. The king lets her in, and the queen puts her to the test.

Sisters, how many times, when getting ready to go to an event or place where potential single men might be, have we taken extra care ahead of time to decide on an outfit? Won't we get a new shirt to go with those jeans that fit just right and show our shape, borrow a pair of shoes to hit off that dress, or run by Charming Charlie's to get the accessories to uplift the outfit? We want our hair done the day of, that fresh from the beauty shop look. We want to put ourselves 'out there' in the sea as attractive specimens waiting to be hooked. There's nothing wrong with us taking care of the bodies our God gave us and "keeping ourselves up." But, let's not stress over physically attracting him. We do that so much. We may even look at our other sisters to determine…what is it about her that I don't have that attracts him to her?

It doesn't matter what has him with her at this moment. IF he is yours, something will be wrong, something not quite right, and his spirit and soul will know that. God will not let the man He has appointed for you tarry elsewhere too long. He'll reveal to that man that he's looking in the wrong spot, or God will throw up a block that makes that man detour, and eventually, he'll leave there. Remember, though, that we are talking about a man seeking a wife-not a right-now girlfriend-kinda situation.

In **Genesis 24**, Abraham has sent his servant on a quest for Isaac's wife. The servant has to journey before finding the right one. Abraham sends him to his homeland to find one of his kindred, and the servant prays to God for a sign of who the right young woman is for Isaac.

The man God has for you will be praying to Him for a sign, girls.

The Bible says that while the servant was yet praying before he was even done speaking in prayer, "Rebekah came out!" Yaasss! She "came out" and didn't even know her moment with destiny was there. Just being the woman of God that she was and unbeknownst to the servant's prayer, she drew water from the well and gave it to the servant and his camels-just as the servant had asked for a sign! The servant held his peace, watched her as she did her work, and then enquired who her people were.

The man looking at you may be holding his peace while he's trying to discern if you are the one or not. So don't let the quietness or lack of moving your way get you down.

In conversation, she revealed she was Abraham's kindred, confirming the servant's answer, and he began to worship. When God reveals that you are chosen for THE MAN He has created for you, He will feel indebted to God so much that it will cause him to praise and worship God for you. But, on the other hand, if the man you are looking at and may even be feeling *does not see you as a God-given gift*, you are not for Him.

Also, note, ladies, Rebekah didn't have to flaunt who she was, speak on her character, or post quotes on social media, trying to put something out there to appear spiritual or philosophical, either. The jewel of who she was shone through by just being her usual self. If your 'normal self' is of value, your aura will let everyone in the room know it. After the servant spoke with Rebekah, she ran to her mother's household and told them.

Ladies, we tell too many people our business, not in our inner circle. Only your inner circle, who has your best interest at heart, needs to know anything.

When the servant came to Rebekah's father's house, he wouldn't even eat without letting them know the business at hand. Isaac needed a wife, and Rebekah was who he wanted for Isaac.

Any man who keeps putting off meeting your family or who has no interest in coming soon with his intentions towards you-well, he might not be the one.

Rebekah's family knew the doing was of the Lord. So they blessed it-another confirmation. At the end of the chapter, we find that Isaac is in the field meditating when he lifts his eyes and sees Rebekah coming, then makes her his wife.

Verse 67-And Isaac brought her into his mother Sarah's tent, and took Rebekah, and she became his wife; and he loved her: and Isaac was comforted after his mother's death.

I know we can't see it yet, but THE MAN will place you as the lady of the house. He will love you, and you alone will be his comfort. I know it sounds redundant, but in the meantime, be about your Heavenly Father's business becoming the princess He wants you to be. Like Rebekah and even the Princess in the Fairy Tale, you won't have to jump through hoops of fire. Your rightful position will be revealed, and no one else can have it. If someone else has it, then it's not yours.

Times may present with what seems like despair. Everyone else is dating and getting boyfriends, marrying, jumping from one relationship to another, shacking with their fiancé, etc. You are trying your best to do right but getting no signs of anything coming your way. Keep on being God's princess. Trust Him to lead you to the right gate at the right time, and THE MAN will find you.

Let's pray…

God, I pray for my single sisters right now. You designed us with a natural longing to be with a man. We often try to attach to the side of ribs that you did not create us to fit with. For that, Lord, we are sorry. Forgive us for seeking with flesh and not in the Spirit. I pray right now for my sister reading this that the effects of any unhealthy or soul-tie attachments that were not of you be diminished. Reveal to us what we were to learn from those relationships, but do not allow any leftover scar tissue to remain. Dissect what you need to dissect. Do an incision and drain any infection that has been able to reside in our hearts, minds, and souls after ill contact. Jesus, we know you to be the balm in Gilead to heal sin-sick souls. Be the master surgeon of our beings right now, Lord, and heal us! Arm our system with protection from any demonic organisms that might try to enter again, causing recurring infection. You have the power to make us new, and we call on that power right now, Lord. Your daughters are crying for the helpmates you intend for us to have for the purpose of your kingdom. Help us to remain steadfast as jewels, women of God worthy of the calling of a wife. Help us remain steadfast in the hope that you will move at the speed of purpose. Help us to remain steadfast in our current purpose until that change comes. We bless you for hearing our cries and trust you and your plan. In Jesus' name, we pray. Amen. Thank you, Lord, for our blessing.

VII

THE CONCLUSION OF THE MATTER

DEVOTION 21:FROM ASHES TO BEAUTY

"The Spirit of the Lord GOD is upon Me, Because the LORD has anointed Me To preach good tidings to the poor; He has sent Me to heal the brokenhearted, To proclaim liberty to the captives, And the opening of the prison to those who are bound; To proclaim the acceptable year of the LORD, And the day of vengeance of our God; To comfort all who mourn, To console those who mourn in Zion, To give them beauty for ashes, The oil of joy for mourning, The garment of praise for the spirit of heaviness; That they may be called trees of righteousness, The planting of the LORD, that He may be glorified." - Isaiah 61:1-3 (New King James Version)

This book was written to give a spark of hope to women in "seemingly" broken times. I used the word "seemingly" on purpose. I wanted to impress upon us all that the season we are in, whether causing sadness, confusion, frustration, or distress- it's only a season. Whatever is going on, my hope is that you realize your situation is not forever broken. Do not deem it a 'Humpty Dumpty can never be put together again' kind of situation. Doing so dismisses your position as a daughter of the King of Kings.

I hope you realize our God does His best work when you give him 'less than' to work with. The children of Israel found themselves often in 'less than' situations. In the text of this concluding devotion, Isaiah prophesied to the children of Israel that there was One coming who would comfort them, console them, and give them beauty for ashes. When I meditate on beauty being given for ashes, three things come to mind.

How can we talk about ashes and not mention the girl in the ashes, Cinderella? There are numerous versions of this folktale, but all of them have Cinderella coming from a season of despair. A season where nothing seems as if it will turn for her. But in the most common version, a fairy godmother appears and helps to magically turn things around for her. Even though she has a glimpse of something better at the ball, problems still occur. Disguised, she is limited by the midnight curfew. She is limited by having to hide who she really is. She is limited by not being able to come straight forward and let the prince know the glass slipper belongs to her. But before the story ends, things change. Her season of wallowing in the ashes comes to an end. There is joy, love, and more. There is a royal position that awaits her. There is love overflowing that awaits her. She is given a life of beauty for her ashes.

I also think about gardening when I think about ashes. I in no way have a green thumb, but I have two small flowerpots outside. The soil reminds me of ashes. It is dirty and grimy, but necessary for the gardening process. The seed must go in the ground, the ashes of dirt, and remain for a season.

Depending on the flower, the timing and length of the season vary. But the seed, like Cinderella, remains underneath. The seed remains unnoticed by passers-by. In some ways, it is buried in the soil. The seed experiences a death in the soil, but the death is actually transformation.

Just like the caterpillar metamorphosizes in the cocoon, so does the seed metamorphosize in the ashes of the soil. It takes sunny, rainy, and dry days for the seed to transform. It may even take a little poking and prodding in the soil that may be uncomfortable for the seed. But, oh, when it begins to grow! When the stem spurts out of the ashes with leaves, you know time is coming soon. It yields the most beautiful blossom that you would not have thought could have come from the beginnings of the seed, but that is how beauty comes from ashes.

Then, I am reminded of my Savior. He was misused and abused. Overlooked. Lied on. Neglected. Forsaken. Disappointed by close family and friends. Wrongfully convicted and then mutilated. Tattered and torn was His body on the cross, and He was buried, like a seed, in a cold, dark grave.

There was a season that His enemies taunted Him, talked about Him, and even thought they had won. But He knew that season was not His destiny.

In Mark 9, Jesus told His disciples that He would be killed, but

He would rise again in three days. AND HE DID!!! The cross bore on His shoulders was ashes, but, oh, how beautiful IS His crown!!! He knew He would be victorious over His season, and my sisters, we will be victorious, too!!

In every situation, I want you to know that you have an advocate more powerful than a fairy godmother. You have a High Priest with ALL POWER in His hands advocating for you. When I say in every situation, I literally mean in e-ve-ry, single, solitary situation–even the ones you got yourself in outside of His will, He can and will give you beauty for ashes.

He did it for our sister Ruth. Sister Esther. Sister Sarah. Sister Rachel. Sister Hannah. Sister Mary. Sister Elizabeth. Sister Mary Magdalene. Sister at the Well. AND He will do it for us, too! Y'all, hold on!! Know that this season will end. Yield to His creative power and let the process take place. Surrender to be buried in ashes, if necessary, for His wonder-working power to be performed.

In all his glory, Matthew 6 says that King Solomon was not arrayed as beautiful as a lily in the field. All the lily does is allow itself to be on the potter's wheel in the garden. Surrender your will. Die to self. Allow Him to work with you in the ashes and mold you like clay. Then, when your season is over, sister, let your beauty shine forth! Beauty beyond the broken glass slipper!!!

Let's pray…

Father God, I come to you right now as humbly as I know how. I know I am not worthy of speaking over my sisters, yet you have called me to do so for such a time as this. As I stir the gift within me, God, I pray that my sisters will feel the presence of your Holy Spirit right now in their lives. In the dirt of whatever is going on, let the peace of your Holy Spirit reign, Lord. In the lowest common denominator, we know of ourselves in the Spirit, we give you all our broken pieces, Lord. We give our thoughts, hopes, dreams, and broken glass slippers – the fairy tales that have yet to come to pass. Anything that is fairy tale flesh in our wanting but is not in line with your will for our lives concerning the Kingdom, we ask that you take, Lord. We surrender to you, Lord, every little broken piece of that glass slipper desire. We ask that you transform our minds and renew our spirits, God. Mold and make our heart's desire to be pleasing to You. We know that whatever You have for us is a more extraordinary gift than we could ever imagine. That gift is not so much our heart's desire as it is to be transformed into the women you are creating us to be. Prepare us to handle the gift when it comes. We praise You now, Lord, for our destinies are set in the Heavens. We praise You for making us into gems of precious value higher than we could have imagined for ourselves. We praise You for the process. We praise You for the expected end being exceedingly abundantly above anything we could think or ask for. We praise you for turning our ashes into beauty!! And for that – we praise you forevermore!! In the name of Jesus Christ, our Lord!! It is so!! Hallelujah!! Amen!!!!!

BELIEVE

Psalm 130: 1-5 Out of the depths have I cried unto thee, O LORD. Lord, hear my voice: let thine ears be attentive to the voice of my supplications. If thou, LORD, shouldest mark iniquities, O Lord, who shall stand? But there is forgiveness with thee, that thou mayest be feared. I wait for the LORD, my soul doth wait, and in his word do I hope. (King James Version)

Hebrews 6: 10-15 For God is not unrighteous to forget your work and labour of love, which ye have shewed toward his name, in that ye have ministered to the saints, and do minister. And we desire that every one of you do shew the same diligence to the full assurance of hope unto the end: That ye be not slothful, but followers of them who through faith and patience inherit the promises. For when God made promise to Abraham, because he could swear by no greater, he sware by himself, Saying, Surely blessing I will bless thee, and multiplying I will multiply thee. And so, after he had patiently endured, he obtained the promise. (King James Version)